12 Marriage Safeguards

Twelve safeguards that will build a healthy, passionate, and lasting marriage!

SAMUEL & KATIE DEUTH

ISBN 9798373339537

Special Thanks:

As we wrote this book, it was obvious that this is a culmination of the love, wisdom, guidance, and example of what a healthy marriage is and can be that we have observed over the years! So first, thank you to our parents, George and Jackie Deuth, and Dale and Barb Legare. You brought us into a world of love and commitment and called us to build a marriage on God's Word!

To Pastor Eddie and Tammy Windsor, you modeled a fun and mission-focused marriage and guided us through our crucial dating and engagement seasons!

To Pastor Kevin & Sheila Gerald, you taught us to celebrate our differences rather than attacking them, and you encouraged us to always go there in conversations.

And to our incredible pastors, Jurgen and Leanne Matthesius, you model marriage in such an inspiring, healthy, and attractive way! You have set a high bar for serving and calling out the gold in each other!

Dedication

While we're writing this together, I'm the final editor, so I get to add an extra note to specifically honor my beautiful wife.

Katie, my love, you are beyond compare! You said yes to me when we were young and entrusted your future to me. I don't take that lightly, and I'm so honored to be your husband on this incredible adventure with you!

At the time of publishing this book, we're about 20 years into marriage! It has been an incredible ride! Wild at times, scary, frustrating even, but with God's help, great family and friends, and the principles we learned from the Bible that are in this book, we've built a love and marriage that brings meaning and joy to life! And we've only just begun!

I love you with all my heart!

CONTENTS

"Further, my brothers and sisters, rejoice in the Lord!
It is no trouble for me to write the same things to you again,
and it is a safeguard for you."
Philippians 3:1 NIV

CHAPTER 1

MARRIAGE IS A GIFT

He who finds a wife finds what is good
and receives favor from the Lord.
Proverbs 18:22 NIV

One of my favorite events to be a part of is a wedding; so much life, celebration, and anticipation of a great love story ahead! One of my favorite moments is when the groom first gets a glimpse of his bride! There's something unique and beautiful about those initial moments of the rest of someone's forever commitment to each other. As a pastor, I've been able to officiate many weddings, and with that comes the task of looking for the perfect Bible verses and the right words to say to bring attention to God's heart and purpose for that particular moment. Along the way, I discovered that my favorite verse to read during a wedding is from the book Song of Songs.

come out, and look, you daughters of Zion. Look on King Solomon wearing a crown, the crown with which his mother crowned him on the day of his wedding, ***the day his heart rejoiced.***
Song of Songs 3:11 NIV

The ending line says it all, the wedding day is *the day* the groom and bride's hearts rejoice! It's the moment when your heart feels a sense of coming alive in a way never felt before. This full experience of love and joy is the gift of love that God has given us, expressed through marriage. One of God's greatest gifts to humanity is love, romance, marriage, and intimacy, both in sexual intimacy and in deep human connection found only in a committed union between husband and wife. So don't ever downplay the passion and love in weddings as "unnecessary" or "not something that lasts"; instead, honor it as an authentic glimpse of the love that God has given to humanity. It's a passion to be stirred up and encouraged!

You Complete Me

Have you ever been in an airport and watched those reunions between a dating or married couple? There's something beautiful about seeing people in love being reunited together. I almost get choked up when I see that happen. It's like you're watching them find the other part of themselves! There's an iconic movie line where the man says, "You Complete Me." I grew up hearing all the sermons against that line because pastors were trying to say that you're complete in Christ first and that you don't need to try to make a man or woman complete your brokenness and emptiness. The idea is that we must be two whole people coming together rather than two incomplete halves. Now, I agree with some of that, of course, but if we're not careful, we can diminish the true picture of love, marriage, and the two coming together as one. While your life can be great even if you never marry, there's no doubt that we were designed not to be alone but to come together to be one. So when you choose the man or woman you want to spend the rest of your life with, the person you cannot imagine living without, it really does bring a completeness and wholeness to our lives.

Healthy Relationships Progress

God designed love and romance to mature and lead toward marriage. Unfortunately, our world has distorted love, marriage, and sex, which has led to so much pain and dysfunction. Our world has made commitment and marriage the afterthought rather than the endgame of romance. Life's principles and systems operate best when things are in the correct order and aligned with God's Word. Marriage should be the goal of every romantic relationship between a man and a woman. Because dating leads toward marriage, my parents taught me that we don't start dating someone unless we could see ourselves potentially marrying that person.

Dating should be with the intention of marriage.

Relationships aren't supposed to stay stagnant. If you're dating, it should progress. If you're married, your marriage should be growing. So often, we get in trouble when we attempt to delay the natural flow of a relationship. It can be like trying to swim up a river. So, if you've been dating for years and not progressing in commitment, you may be caught more in a swamp. If your friendship isn't moving towards dating, and from dating to engagement and engagement to marriage and married life to kids and growth in intimacy, then something is off.

It doesn't mean that you have to marry the first person you date, but it means you don't entertain a relationship that you know could never end in marriage because of misaligned values and vision. Only in marriage will a man and a woman fully experience all the love a relationship has to offer. The marriage covenant's strength is what unlocks marriage's full beauty. Marriage is like the fireplace that holds the fires of passion. Within a marriage, you have passion from a few directions. Obviously, sexual intimacy is at the forefront of marriage, but you will also have the forces of tension, anger, pain, and disagreements. These passions are like a fire that will warm the house if it's in the fireplace or burn it down if it's not.

"For this reason a man will leave his father and mother and be united to his wife, and the two will become one flesh." This is a profound mystery—but I am talking about Christ and the church. However, each one of you also must love his wife as he loves himself, and the wife must respect her husband.
Ephesians 5:31-33 NIV

Better Together

In an era celebrating individualism and trying to fight against uniting but emphasizing our difference and separation even after marriage, we're really missing the point. We're designed to operate in strength when we come together. Elements of ourselves being lost within each other is an incredible thing because the two become one. But it's not just a 1+1=2. When we come together, it's multiplication, not addition. Like when a single horse is pulling its weight and then a second horse is added in, it doesn't just double the pulling power; it multiplies it by 10x. So coming together in marriage has the ability to enhance your life greatly! God created and blessed marriage!

Marriage is a Picture and Perfector

Marriage is also a picture of God's commitment and covenant toward us; His commitment to you is forever! God went all-in to seal a partnership with us! So much so that He gave his one and only Son, Jesus, on the cross! With Jesus' death and resurrection, He purchased our salvation and established this covenant, and nothing in heaven or earth can break and stop His love toward us. You can be confident that God won't abandon or leave you for someone else. His covenant with you stands forever! In the same way, marriage is to be a reflection of that covenant and commitment. No matter what comes your way, be fully committed to giving all for each other.

Marriage is also a perfector. There's something powerful about the two becoming one. The process of learning to serve each other and laying down your life for each other is often painful but beautiful in its results. For a marriage to work and be great requires that you each grow. See marriage as a tool God uses to shape you into the masterpiece that He designed you to be. You will create beautiful music together, but the sparks will also fly as you clash! Don't be afraid of the sparks of iron sharpening iron; it's how you get better.

A Note for Our Single Friends

The focus of this book is establishing safeguards for your marriage, but you don't need to wait till marriage begins to prepare for marriage. In fact, the best time to learn these principles and set them in place is before you're married. Of course, these marriage safeguards can be added throughout our marriage journey, but never dismiss marriage insight because you're not yet married. As a single man, I loved messages on marriage and relationships because I knew I was stockpiling wisdom to avoid the pitfalls that often come to sabotage a marriage. So, if you're single, dating, or engaged, take massive notes and make all the highlights you can in this book, and it will set you up with a significant advantage in your marriage!

CHAPTER 2

MARRIAGE IS A COVENANT

'For this reason a man will leave his father and mother and be united to his wife, and the two will become one flesh.' So they are no longer two, but one flesh. Therefore what God has joined together, let no one separate."
Mark 10:7-9 NIV

Marriage is more than a ceremony and honeymoon; it's beyond just a piece of paper and rings; it is a covenant. A marriage covenant is designed to be unbreakable, just as God's covenant with us is. God is the author of marriage and declares that once we enter into marriage, that covenant should never be separated. Your marriage commitment isn't purely based on whether or not your spouse holds up their end of the deal but on your commitment to God first. No matter what your spouse does or doesn't do, my commitment is before God, and I ultimately must answer to God with how I handle the marriage covenant.

The covenant of marriage signifies that we're not just committed to each other when life is good or easy, but through all circumstances that life throws at us. It's why in a wedding ceremony, we use phrases like "for richer or poorer, in sickness and in health, till death do us part." All these phrases speak to a deeper agreement that is beyond personal comfort and circumstantial ease. Since marriage includes two people with different opinions, values systems, family backgrounds, and life experiences, you can be sure that marriage won't be perfect, but when two people are committed to each other, forsaking all others and remaining committed no matter the circumstances, it begins to shape something incredible.

The Deadliest Seven-Letter Word!

One of the critical things to a lasting marriage is establishing a " no escape clause, " whether you're right at the start or you've been married for years. An escape clause is when we leave room for the deadly seven-letter word "Divorce." I find that when we have the option to avoid pain or difficulty, we tend to take it. I knew a couple one time that often joked about giving their marriage a 10-year test run, and then they'd reconsider; well, sadly, they got divorced right as their ten years were up. Don't allow any room for escape. It's time to eliminate the word DIVORCE from our marriage vocabulary. No matter how frustrated, angry, or disappointed you are, don't jump to using the threat of divorce. Let your yes be yes and your no be no. You won't be able to enjoy the intended value of the marriage relationship without being all in.

Burn the Ships!

Maybe you've heard of the icon story of Cortés and the burning of his ships. In the year 1519, Hernán Cortés arrived in the New World with six hundred men and, upon arrival, made history by destroying his ships. This sent a clear message to his men: There is no turning back. And in the same way, on our wedding day, we burn the ships; there is no going back! No return policy on your marriage. I should say that God calls us to a no-return policy. Obviously, our culture preaches a message to ditch your spouse if they aren't making you happy, but God calls us to be fully committed to our spouse until our last breath.

"This is what the Sovereign Lord says: I will deal with you as you deserve because you have despised my oath by breaking the covenant. Yet I will remember the covenant I made with you in the days of your youth, and I will establish an everlasting covenant with you."
Ezekiel 16:59-60 NIV

God uses the covenant of marriage to refer to himself and Israel in the Old Testament and then to Jesus and the Church in the New Testament. And with this parallel, God calls on his people to be committed and not run around on the covenant that has been made. God also showcases an incredible commitment to His people even when they break the covenant. He reached out to them over and over again out of His love and the covenant He had entered into. With God's help, approach your marriage with the same unconditional commitment.

"The days are coming," declares the Lord, "when I will make a new covenant with the people of Israel and with the people of Judah. It will not be like the covenant I made with their ancestors when I took them by the hand to lead them out of Egypt, because they broke my covenant, though I was a husband to them," declares the Lord. "This is the covenant I will make with the people of Israel after that time," declares the Lord. "I will put my law in their minds and write it on their hearts. I will be their God, and they will be my people.
Jeremiah 31:31-33 NIV

CHAPTER 3

MARRIAGE IS A CATALYST

As iron sharpens iron, so one person sharpens another.
Proverbs 27:17 NIV

Can two people walk together without agreeing on the direction?
Amos 3:3 NLT

A catalyst is something that is introduced to create change and or to accelerate progress. Marriage is a catalyst; it will instigate change and acceleration in your life! During our single years, there are so many things that God teaches us and develops in us, but there are new lessons and new ways that he challenges us and transforms us through marriage. The primary experience of marriage is the gift of love and connection, and the secondary is the function of shaping and purifying our lives. Nothing in my world brings me more face-to-face with my areas of dysfunction than marriage. This can be scary, but if you open up your life and heart, you'll find that your spouse is perfectly designed to help you overcome those areas. Marriage is the only place strong enough to secure us while we're in that perfecting state.

The question is whether or not I'll allow marriage to do in me what God designed it to do. Will I allow my spouse to speak into my world? Will I allow the tension of two imperfect people coming together to teach me the lessons of grace, forgiveness, mercy, and strength that it's designed to teach? Or will I push against the lessons and remain unchanged?

Mirror, Mirror on the Wall

Marriage also has a way of being like a mirror; it's an honest reflection of where I'm at in life. In marriage, I come face to face with my Selfishness. It's wild how much the center of your own world you can become in the single years, which gets confronted when God introduces another x factor into your world! Having to share your life with your husband or wife forces you to start thinking about others. I also see reflected back at me all my insecurities. What your husband or wife does or says will start triggering areas you've been able to avoid. Learning how to lead, submit, and love each other brings all kinds of insecurities and fears to the surface. We will for sure come face to face with the dysfunctions of our family upbringing and ideologies. We all have very different families, and no home is perfect. But you'll have to learn to grow when your spouse questions, "Why do you keep doing that?"

Your Spouse has what You Need!

The Bible calls Eve, Adam's helpmate because our spouse is our partner and greatest source of strength on earth. If you're open to it, your husband or wife will be the perfect help you need to mature and grow into your calling. My pastor, Jurgen Matthesius, tells a hilarious and confronting story about the early years of their marriage. He was unhappy with how his wife, Leanne, was acting, and she had finally had enough of his name-calling that she threatened divorce. So, in a tantrum, he went to God to pray and complain about her, which didn't end up being a good move! Ha! As he was praying, God asked him, "What kind of wife would you like to have?" Jurgen was pumped about that question and started listing things like, "I'd like her to carry herself like a princess." God replied to him by asking, "When's the last time you called her a princess?" And my pastor responded with, "When she acts like a princess, then I'll start calling her one and treating her like one." At that moment, he felt the Holy Spirit say,

"Your wife is a product of your husbandry."

This was to say that if you want a princess, you need to start calling her one and treating her like one, even before she's acting like one. The truth is that we form with our words, and as a husband or wife, we have the extreme privilege to help shape and encourage our spouse. The truth is, if you don't like what you see in your spouse, then change what you're saying to your spouse.

Focus on the Good

Marriage experts Les and Leslie Parrott once said, "Opposites Attract, and then they attack." If we're not careful, what's meant to be a union designed to bring life can then move to bring death. The reasons that brought the two of you together can gradually become the things that frustrate you if you let them. You can stop that before it starts, or if you feel your marriage has gotten toxic, you can begin to encourage each other again instead of attacking each other.

Finally, brothers and sisters, whatever is true, whatever is noble, whatever is right, whatever is pure, whatever is lovely, whatever is admirable—if anything is excellent or praiseworthy —think about such things.
Philippians 4:8 NIV

You'll find that marriage doesn't just shine a light on all the uncomfortable places but also becomes, or has the potential to become, the most significant source of strength. Marriage will bring out your callings and passions. You must see part of your role as calling out the gold in your spouse. It may sometimes feel like the gold and diamonds are covered in dirt, but keep digging and stay focused on the diamonds, not the dirt. Your spouse is amazing; they are a gift from God!

No Strings Attached

When you marry someone, you can't marry them with conditions of change. While we want to grow, and marriage will certainly cause you to grow if you let it; our love for people cannot be dependent on change. Trying to build a marriage with strings attached can create major points of frustration and dissatisfaction. When you set up your relationship to only work as long as your spouse meets all your needs and makes you happy more than they frustrate you, it's easy for the marriage to move into manipulation and dysfunction.

It's time to cut the strings and love freely and without conditions!

Our commitment to our spouse is till death do us part, even if no change or growth transpires. But, I want to challenge you to make a commitment to yourself and to your spouse that you will continue to grow and develop and become all that you've been called to be and that you'll commit to helping support your spouse to becoming what God has called them to be as well.

CHAPTER 4

MARRIAGE HOLDS THE FUTURE

"Love the Lord your God with all your heart and with all your soul and with all your strength. These commandments that I give you today are to be on your hearts. Impress them on your children. Talk about them when you sit at home and when you walk along the road, when you lie down and when you get up. Tie them as symbols on your hands and bind them on your foreheads. Write them on the doorframes of your houses and on your gates."
Deuteronomy 6:5-9 NIV

Have you ever created a time capsule? You put unique things inside a container, then bury them for a future time and generation to discover. Marriage is also a time capsule for the future. Within the marriage covenant, God places the most beautiful treasures of little children inside the marriage to be covered and protected so they can grow and be opened up at a future time. The strength and structural health of the time capsule determine if the treasures stayed intact; in the same way, the marriage's strength will determine the children's health. The children are the fruit and future of your marriage. I've written more about this in my book, *Seven Biblical Principles on Parenting.*

In the beginning, God gives a mission to Adam and Eve by telling them to increase, multiply, and fill the whole earth. Marriage and family are the only vessels we have to fulfill this call by God, and by the way, this mandate still exists. Part of the langue of that mandate is to subdue and take dominion. Our families are "the way" we fill and extend the purpose and kingdom of God on earth. The future preachers, politicians, artists, teachers, actors, parents, business owners, and all people that are key to a strong society are just waiting to be born into a family! Several times in the Bible, God would send a leader in response to the challenges of that hour, and those leaders all came through a family. God would send an angel to announce the child they would have and what to do, like in Sampson's story. He was a response of Heaven, and God entrusted this future deliverer into the hands of a family. My mom, Jackie Deuth, has said many times over the years that she often felt God would remind her how incredibly important her role as a mom was in shaping and preparing her children—knowing that God had entrusted her kids to her and my dad's care. I like to remind her that the impact of our lives as kids gets largely credited to my parent's account.

Healthy Home, Strong Nation.

While I get into marriage out of love and passion, and my family builds out of personal intimacy, we also have to understand that our marriages and homes are not just for ourselves alone. Your marriage is the incubator and holder of the future of the nation God has placed you in.

The health of your home determines the strength of the future.

The importance of the family unit of the father, mother, and children is so essential because the home is where the future begins and is established. Your marriage and the home you create together becomes the model and template for your kids to build their homes. Good or bad, you become the template for them to follow. And collectively, the houses in a community set the climate for that communities schools, businesses, arts, and justice systems. This is also why the enemy goes so hard after destroying the marriage and family unit. The family structure of the father, mother, and children is not some social construct; it's the Biblical model and framework that God has given us for fulfillment and effectiveness. Don't allow the culture you live in to redefine the family as God has designed it. No other combination is designed for life, health, and strength. No other family setup besides the Biblical model can create a strong nation and future.

CHAPTER 5

MARRIAGE NEEDS SAFEGUARDS

"Further, my brothers and sisters, rejoice in the Lord!
It is no trouble for me to write the same things to you again,
and it is a safeguard for you."
Philippians 3:1 NIV

We usually come to marriage deeply in love and consumed with each other and all the beauty of the season, and you should! But, in all those emotions, we usually don't plan ahead to protect this incredible marriage commitment because we assume it to be unbreakable or unshakable. But, when you purchase an expensive vehicle or technology, you usually also purchase an insurance plan to help you best protect this valuable asset. In the same way, we must protect our most important earthly relationship, which is our marriage. Sadly, a couple usually doesn't realize the need for this until their marriage is so off track that it feels beyond saving. That is why your marriage needs something to guard it and keep it safe and strong. Another way to look at it is when you have precious valuables at home; you usually keep them protected in a safe or guarded by a security system. Yet, the most precious thing on earth, MARRIAGE, is often left unguarded and open for attack and decay.

A Healthy and passionate marriage will not stay that way by accident; we must SAFEGUARD our marriage.

ˈsāfˌgärd –

- **Noun:** a measure taken to protect someone or something or to prevent something undesirable.
- **Verb:** protect from harm or damage with an appropriate measure.
- **Synonyms:** protection, defense, guard, screen, buffer, preventive, precaution, provision, security

You'll notice that a Safeguard is a measure that must be thought of ahead of time. It's less reactionary and more an intentional advanced strategy to be sure your relationship remains healthy for the long haul. We must decide ahead of time to implement habits and practices that SAFEGUARD and create a healthy marriage. If you're reading this book, chances are high that you want to build a significant and lasting marriage. So commit right now with your spouse or future spouse that you will commit to putting in the work to change, grow, and set up these twelve safeguards together.

Most wait till their marriage is rocky to try and figure things out, but what if you could put in SAFEGUARDS that would keep your marriage safe and ensure that you have a fun, healthy, and passionate marriage for years to come? Also, Safeguards aren't just about "not getting a divorce." They are about creating a thriving love story together. And while this book is valuable if you're beginning in marriage, know that these safeguards can be installed into your marriage at any point to strengthen or restore life and health. Some of these safeguards were taught to my wife and me before marriage, many were learned along the way, and for sure, all of them were things we had to grow in as we went. As for Katie and I, our marriage is in a place of health and strength at the time of writing this book, but for it to continue in health, we must keep embracing these safeguards. These principles aren't just one-time applications but an ongoing commitment.

All of us can have a great and thriving marriage!

Safeguards are like guardrails for our marriages. On a road trip, you won't find guardrails on every part of the road, just the windy corners and sections where you could end up going off the edge. And usually, those guardrails are sadly there because someone previously went off the road in that area, so now they put up rails. In the same way, we can put safeguards up for our marriage based on our past mistakes and by looking at how others have gone off the rails in their marriages. I don't want to only learn from my mistakes; I want to learn from others and set up my marriage for strength.

"Further, my brothers and sisters, rejoice in the Lord!
It is no trouble for me to write the same things to you again,
and it is a safeguard for you."
Philippians 3:1 NIV

Marriage has Enemies

Now, on the road, the guardrails are there usually because of someone accidentally going over the edge, but in our marriages, it's not just the things that accidentally happen; there are also some intentional enemies of our marriages that we must be smart about. Marriage has three specific enemies that are attempting to stop it.

1. *Supernatural:*

The devil wants to destroy marriages because it destroys the image of God and destroys the future! The devil is about shortcutting future potential. While not every struggle in your marriage is because of demonic influence, you do want to be sure that you are aware of the enemy's desire to bring division to your marriage. The Bible says that the devil is like a roaring lion, looking for someone to devour, but you don't have to become another divorce stat.

2. *Internal Forces:*

Enemies from within. These are just the combination of my personal life issues. My attitudes, upbringing, experiences, temptations, and choices. When we come to marriage, we all bring some level of baggage from our past that must be dealt with. This is also our greatest area for accountability and ownership. You won't be able to guard and keep your marriage healthy if you don't take full ownership of the areas you are self-sabotaging your marriage. The good news is that we can all change and grow!

3. *External Factors:*

Outside enemies. There are many Outside factors and life pressures, like money, tragedies, and people. Be aware of and intentional with the inputs you allow to enter your marriage.

This book is designed then to help us Safeguard against the natural and supernatural enemies of our marriages. This book is geared toward married people as well as couples still dating or engaged. The sooner you begin to set up these principles in your life, the better off your marriage will be!

CHAPTER 6

SAFEGUARD #1
TRUSTING GOD'S WORD

Trust in the Lord with all your heart and lean not on your own understanding; in all your ways submit to him, and he will make your paths straight.
Proverbs 3:5-6 NIV

As we set off on this journey of setting up safeguards for a healthy and strong marriage, or if you're working on breathing life back into your relationship, it's vital that we begin with the ultimate authority on relationships which is God himself. There are many different opinions and voices that want to speak into your relationship; some of them may be family members, well-meaning friends, or colleagues, but if we're going to last the distance in our relationship, then we must build our lives and marriages on the solid foundation of God's word.

Anchors and Foundations

When your relationship faces a storm like finances or health, you need something that can stabilize you in the storm. That's why we need anchors and a solid foundation. An anchor keeps our home steady while the storm is raging, and the foundation is what we build the home on. Jesus tells a story of a wise and foolish builder.

"Therefore everyone who hears these words of mine and puts them into practice is like a wise man who built his house on the rock. The rain came down, the streams rose, and the winds blew and beat against that house; yet it did not fall, because it had its foundation on the rock. But everyone who hears these words of mine and does not put them into practice is like a foolish man who built his house on sand. The rain came down, the streams rose, and the winds blew and beat against that house, and it fell with a great crash."
Matthew 7:24-27 (NIV)

This is such a powerful illustration Jesus is giving us and is the perfect truth for us in building marriages and families. The marriage is the center of every home; the strength of the marriage will determine the health and strength of the rest of the house. You'll notice that this parable that Jesus is teaching is focused on his beginning phrase of *Hearing and Applying God's Word.* In the same way, if we don't have the word of God infused as the key ingredient in the foundation of our marriage, we'll build on the weak and constantly shifting sands of culture and our emotions.

God's Way vs. The Culture

Many reading this book have likely grown up in nations where you're used to not being "controlled" or restricted. So, we can see something or someone telling us what we can or cannot do in relationships as a cosmic killjoy, but all of God's Biblical boundaries for marriage are for your good. Submission to God's Word unlocks the health of your personal and married life rather than destroying it. His word is the final truth and holds the best practices for us in our communication, sexuality, work, play, purpose, and many other areas of our life and marriage. The Bible isn't just a guide for getting to heaven someday; it's also the guide for bringing heaven to earth today! Some are on their way to heaven, but their marriage and other relationships feel like hell, but you don't need to settle for that. Maybe you've only seen dysfunction in the marriages around you, but let us encourage you that marriage can be heaven on earth! For this to happen, we must follow and apply God's Word to our lives, not the latest ideas from a sinful world.

At most grocery stores, there's usually some magazine headline telling you the latest tips and tricks to a better relationship or sex life, but let me strongly encourage you not to pick those up for advice; instead, go to God's tried and true formula.

When you enter the land the Lord your God is giving you, do not learn to imitate the detestable ways of the nations there.
Deuteronomy 18:9 NIV

Remember that everything the devil tries to feed us is a counterfeit version of God's good plans and design. The culture will try to tell you how to have a great relationship, but the world has no track record worthy of following. So don't try to shape your marriage according to culture. If you do, it will end up distorted rather than shaped into something beautiful.

Do not conform to the pattern of this world, but be transformed by the renewing of your mind. Then you will be able to test and approve what God's will is—his good, pleasing and perfect will.
Romans 12:2 (NIV)

For example, Culture downplays marriage, but God says it's a good thing! Culture says to live together and sleep together before marriage, but the Bible says to wait until marriage. Culture says "love is love" and endorses same-sex relationships, but God designed marriage to be between one biological man and woman. If you are reading this book and happen to find yourself in any of those unbiblical scenarios, it doesn't mean that God loves you less, but it does mean you are heading for relational and potentially eternal heartache. However, the good news is that you have choices. You can choose to go with your feelings and culture or choose to run in the direction of the word of God and surrender your life to it. God's way will always lead to life and health!

Let Emotions Indicate, Not Lead.

In our marriages, emotions make great indicators but poor guides. When emotions flair up in your spouse, don't let emotions take the reins and ruin your night; instead, stop and speak life and healing to that point of hurt or pain that the emotions are highlighting. In marriage, we each have to learn to stop and assess our spouse's emotions to determine what is really behind them. When I do that, I can focus more on helping than hurting by reacting emotionally. We don't need to dismiss emotions, but we don't need to be a slave to them either. I have to learn to submit my feelings and emotions ultimately to the truth. My emotions are how I feel but may not always be what is true. You must have something that can trump your emotions; the Bible and His truth are the ultimate authority, and we want to pass all of our thoughts, emotions, and philosophies through the Word of God. In your marriage, you need to force your emotions to submit to what is true about your spouse or that circumstance. You may feel your spouse is unloving or not there for you, but stop and look back over your marriage and uncover the truth. The truth most likely is that your husband or wife has done many things to show their love and appreciation towards you, but at this moment, the emotions are causing those good memories to fade, but they are the truth. In our marriage, when I felt like my wife wasn't encouraging or trusting me, it would send me down a spiral of feeling like she didn't love me and that maybe she's "always" been like this. But then I'd run those emotions through the truth filter by looking at the history of our marriage to see that's not true and also that my wife had grown in those areas as well.

Everyone wants to feel happy in their marriage, and I believe that everyone can feel that or be on their way towards more feelings of love, joy, and romance in marriage, but the question is, when you don't feel happy in life or your relationships, what is your instinctive response? Is it to do things like blame, run, ignore, or hide? Most often, our instinct response comes from how we learned emotional management in our families, which is why you need to work together with your spouse to deal with and confront your emotions in a way that brings healing and health. For example, when Katie and I were first married, and we'd get into a challenging argument, she had the instinct to say, "Maybe we shouldn't have gotten married." She wouldn't say we should get divorced, but she saw all conflict as a major red flag. This came from assuming that if I was having a tough conversation, that meant that I didn't love her. But, I was taught that all relationships move forward as we face challenges and emotions and work through them. The presence of pain and emotions doesn't mean something is wrong. One of my friends and marriage therapists that my wife and I go to said:

"If you're fighting in your marriage
that means your marriage is working."
Dr. Brian Reiswig

Be careful of making feelings the king of your life. You see, the challenge with making my personal happiness my ultimate goal and the thing that I will do whatever is necessary to achieve is that I unintentionally start doing the opposite things to what will actually make me happy. This verse shows us that pursuing good for others is how we find good coming to us.

"Do nothing out of selfish ambition or vain conceit. Rather, in humility value others above yourselves, not looking to your own interests but each of you to the interests of the others."
Philippians 2:3-4 (NIV)

This is one of the key verses in the Bible that we must submit our emotions to if we actually want to experience the joys and benefits of relationship and marriage. When my spouse doesn't make me happy, I have a choice to retaliate and manipulate the scenario to get what I want or stay focused on my commitment to serve and hold up my side of the marriage as Jesus set the example for us to do. We've definitely been caught in that dysfunctional cycle plenty of times. This is one of marriage's most iconic and vicious cycles, and one of the two has to walk in humility to stop it from spiraling down to a crash. Humility and maturity is realizing that while it might feel like my spouse isn't meeting my needs, I'm going to recognize that's not a personal attack on me but is most likely a response to pain or hurt in their life— my role is to focus more on finding the gap and filling it rather than withholding love until I get what I want.

Two Things We Must Do with Emotions

There are plenty of things you don't want to do with negative emotions, the main one being reacting or acting out on them every time. But here are two key things we need to do to correctly use emotions to strengthen our marriage rather than allowing them to destroy it.

1. Use emotions to highlight your own areas of insecurity, pain, or brokenness.

Too many want to instantly blame everyone else for their emotional state of sadness, loneliness, or anger, but what my wife and I try to do is let those emotions prompt us to ask, "Why am I feeling and reacting this way?"

Our instinct is to think, "I'm feeling this way because you did ______," but most of the time, it's because of an issue, stress, or an unresolved area of my life that's not been dealt with. If we can learn not to be "triggered" by our spouse but instead to use the emotions to trigger us to dig in and identify where that frustration is coming from, it will keep us in a team player mindset. It also allows us to invite our spouse into our world and healing process.

See your spouse not as your enemy but as your advocate in the healing process.

2. Use Emotions to cause you to change how you love your spouse. Usually, my frustration and emotion come from a need I have that I feel my spouse isn't meeting. So, I can either attack and try to manipulate my wife/husband to try and force them to meet my need, which never really works. Or I can ask why my spouse isn't automatically wanting to fulfill that need I have. For example, in our marriage, I would be frustrated that my wife wasn't more affectionate or more willing to have sex whenever I wanted it. I tried initially to manipulate her into it, and I'm embarrassed to admit I even used the Bible to try and convince her why it was wrong to deny me, and as you can imagine, that worked really well!! Ha! Eventually, I learned (and still learning) to try and figure out what was going on in my wife's world that was causing her not to be open to me. When I turned my attention off just "my needs" and considered what "her needs were," that's when she began to actually open up. And that's what the Bible teaches us to do; consider the needs of our spouse before ourselves. The world would try to tell you to pursue your happiness as the primary focus in your marriage, and if they don't make you happy, move on to someone else who will, but God says to focus more on your spouse's happiness and fulfillment than your own. There's no biblical precedence for ending a marriage because you're not happy.

Choose to Love

When I was young, I remember my mom would play marriage seminar videos at home as background noise while she worked. One particular time I remember overhearing some old VHS videos of a Gary Smalley marriage conference. One quote that's imprinted into my memory is, "Love is a Discission." Of course, the attraction to your spouse begins in the emotional side of things, and it should! Being captured by her beauty or being captivated by his courage is a wonderful part of the relational start and sparks! But, if you see your marriage as being entirely held together by emotions, there will come a time in your relationship when those emotions are gone, or the feelings of passion have grown colder; it's in those moments where the choice and decision to love is what carries you through.

When we choose God's way in marriage, it will cause us to push through difficult times in a marriage that we may otherwise have decided to throw in the towel. And for us, with nearly twenty years of marriage, you find the richness of marriage continues to grow with time as we overcome adversities in life and marriage. Like a fine wine that gets better with age, marriage has the same ability. The vintage of your relationship only gets better with time!

Love Moves Beyond Words

It can be easy to leave love to just words. However, learning to express your love for each other is so important. Depending on your personality or upbringing, this can be more or less difficult, but we all need to learn to express love verbally to each other. Having said that, all love must move beyond words to action.

Little children (believers, dear ones), let us not love [merely in theory] with word or with tongue [giving lip service to compassion], but in action and in truth [in practice and in sincerity, because practical acts of love are more than words].
1 John 3:18 Amplified Bible

Three Ways to Put Love into Action

1. Plan to spend time together

You may have heard it said that love is spelled TIME. There's a lot of truth to this. We must learn to prioritize each other and be intentional about spending quality time together. This is where a weekly date night can be huge. But, even if there's not an official weekly time, be intentional about connecting consistently. One way to think of this is not to give each other your leftovers. Be careful not to give all your best time, attention, and energy to everyone else but your spouse. I would often do this to my wife and kids by giving all my energy to work or everyone else in social settings. It took some bold and loving confrontation from my wife to remind me to keep the main things the main thing.

2. Find out what the other enjoys

Don't be so self-indulged that it's all about you and what you enjoy. Find out your spouse's favorite foods, activities, movies, and music. Then, be intentional to choose activities that your spouse is excited about. For example, I love seeing a movie in the theater, but Katie's not a big fan because it puts her to sleep. So, I don't push her to go to the movies because I know that's not on the list of what she likes. But she also knows I enjoy that, so she'll rally and enjoy a movie with me. Movies she joins tend to be the animated films that our kids enjoy. Ha!

3. Celebrate Each other

Don't become the old married couple that stops celebrating birthdays and special holidays. Till your last breath, celebrate your wife or husband's birthday! Keep celebrating your anniversary. Zig Ziglar once said, "Anniversaries are boring, so my wife and I just keep having honeymoons." These moments matter and keep you honoring your spouse. When you honor, celebrate, and appreciate your spouse, you'll find that your love, passion, and commitment will continue to grow.

CHAPTER 7

SAFEGUARD #2
COMMITTING TO GROWTH

for giving prudence to those who are simple, knowledge and discretion to the young— let the wise listen and add to their learning, and let the discerning get guidance—
Proverbs 1:4-5 NIV

Earlier, we encouraged you to marry who someone already is, not what they can become, so that you don't enter marriage from a place of wishing your spouse was something they aren't. However, to maintain a healthy and strong marriage, both individuals must be committed to continual growth.

"For this very reason, make every effort to add to your faith goodness; and to goodness, knowledge; and to knowledge, self-control; and to self-control, perseverance; and to perseverance, godliness; and to godliness, mutual affection; and to mutual affection, love. For if you possess these qualities in increasing measure, they will keep you from being ineffective and unproductive in your knowledge of our Lord Jesus Christ. But whoever does not have them is nearsighted and blind, forgetting that they have been cleansed from their past sins. Therefore, my brothers and sisters, make every effort to confirm your calling and election. For if you do these things, you will never stumble,"
2 Peter 1:5-10 NIV

Stay in a learning and growing posture. Don't stop learning about your spouse. Don't stop developing your personal and public self. Don't stop growing your business and finances. Don't stop growing your communication. Don't stop being willing to take input and advice. Be committed to growth and continue to invite the input of others around you.

Take Ownership of Your Marriage Growth

As I noted earlier in the book, one of the greatest marriage lessons that Pastor Jurgen passed along is the revelation from God that our wives are a product of our husbandry.

Your wife is a product of your husbandry.
And your husband flourishes off your words.

It's not always easy to embrace this concept because it means we have to own our marriage issues and growth. It's easier to try and blame issues or dysfunction on your spouse rather than realize that God gave you to your spouse to encourage, serve, and strengthen. So, if your wife isn't growing, you need to take ownership of that; if your husband isn't growing, you need to take ownership of supporting their growth.

Create A Space And Place For Growth.

A key reason people get stuck is because of the fear of failure. We get nervous to step out of our comfort zone because of the concern of what people might think, specifically what our spouse says. So, to ease that concern, it's essential that you commit to creating an atmosphere where you can both try, fail, and get back up again. Don't rub past failures in their face. If you do, you'll send a message that they need to keep quiet and not try again. How you respond when your husband or wife finally steps out to express love or grow in any way is important.

I'm a words-of-affirmation guy, and as you may suspect, I married my opposite, so it was difficult for Katie to express words of affirmation when we were first married. But, because my wife is amazing, she continued to grow in this area, which I wanted to encourage. So, I don't downplay the note she writes in a card or those initial awkward attempts at more verbally expressive love; I celebrate and appreciate her where she is in that growth journey. In the same way, I appreciate her grace when I awkwardly try to plan genuine quality time moments. But here's the truth: you'll get more of what you honor and celebrate in your marriage. So, be each other's biggest fan and cheerleader, and watch how they will continue to grow!

Be Patient with Each Other

Learn to be patient while your spouse grows. You are a key part of helping support or even speed up that growth process, but ultimately, we all grow at different paces, and we must learn to have patience for each other, or we'll get frustrated. There may be areas where you wish they were further along, but trying to rush and push won't always be the right move. Instead, learn to have discernment in when to push and when to be patient. Now, specifically for the men, there may be times you get frustrated with some area where your wife isn't meeting an expectation, but if you're honest, you most likely haven't helped provide an atmosphere for her to grow in that area. I know I've fallen prey to that reality in our marriage, and then God would remind me that the harvest in my wife's life is a result of the seeds I'm sowing.

Five Areas We Need to Keep Growing In

1. Communication

We're different, and that's how God designed it. Part of our differences in communication can feel like it pushes us away from each other, but God wants you to use that difference to keep you growing and figuring each other out. One of you may need more processing time than the other, but that's ok, learn to flow with it. One of you may like more direct and straight to the point, and the other is looking for more of the sandwich method; neither is more right, and the key is that you continue to communicate. Be attentive to what opens up or shuts down your spouse in a conversation. If you learn to be attentive to each other, you'll start increasing good communication and decreasing the triggers that shut each other down.

2. Problem-Solving

In marriage, you'll have challenges you come up against or differences that seem to be insurmountable. Don't let any challenge be too great; commit to problem-solving and growing together. And don't see problem-solving as one winning and the other losing, but learn to work together to come to solutions where you both win. Sometimes compromise will need to be a part of coming to an agreement. But both of you need to be mindful that it's not always one of you compromising their preference for the other. When is the last time you let your spouse have it their way?

3. Finances

Yes, you want to keep growing your income and wealth creation, but in this case, I'm specifically speaking about keeping the lines of communication open and partnering together in your finances. Money is often one of the most significant stress points in marriage. We dealt with this and have had many iterations because of it. Because my wife is more detailed, at first, my wife mostly handled our budget, but when we went through a difficult time financially, it created unhealthy pressure on my wife, so I took it over. Now it's more of a partnership. There are several budgeting apps and resources to help you set up your life and marriage for success.

4. *Serving Each Other*

Keep learning to notice and meet the needs of your spouse. I know this isn't easy because our spouse's needs are less instinctive than our own, but the reward is always in the sacrifice. Serving is always the way forward in all areas of our lives. Serving is selfless, which is often counterintuitive, but if you keep working to fulfill each other's needs, you'll be shocked at how much growth will take place. As a note, this doesn't mean that you're always doing whatever your spouse wants—often serving means that you're doing what is needed, not always what is wanted. Husbands and wives carry different key roles within a marriage, and part of the way we serve each other is by playing our roles—husbands as leaders and providers and women as helpmates and creating a life-giving home atmosphere.

5. *Showing Affection*

All marriages start with passion and love like a blazing fire! But, over time, it can die out if we don't keep stoking the fire. So keep showing small displays of love and affection, as well as make time for consistent sexual intimacy. We'll talk more about this in a later chapter but don't allow yourself to downplay physical affection. It's not an optional extra; it's central to a thriving marriage. Hold hands, kiss often, cuddle, and have as much sex as possible!

Marriage Dies When We Settle

We'll end this focus on growth by reminding us all to keep growing and never settle! Don't settle for a marriage that's "just getting by." Your marriage will stall out and begin to plummet if the two of you stop growing. But, if you keep growing, so will your marriage. Till death do you part! Commit to helping each other grow till your very last breath.

CHAPTER 8

SAFEGUARD #3 HEALTHY & HONEST COMMUNICATION

Wounds from a friend can be trusted,
but an enemy multiplies kisses.
Proverbs 27:6

At the beginning of our marriage, I made a commitment and decision that I'm not even sure I understood the power of at the time. I decided that no matter what we faced, I would "go there" in conversations, even if it was uncomfortable. This meant that if I needed, I'd rather go sleep on the couch because we were in a fight rather than ignore the elephant in the room. Thankfully, through all the difficult moments in our marriage, Katie has never tried to send me to the couch, at least not yet! Well, except maybe from my snoring. (pray for her) There were many times in the early years when we hadn't resolved something before bed, and I was going to sleep, and my wife couldn't sleep and would head out to the couch. In those moments, I'd either decide to enjoy more room in the bed or do the hard work of getting out of bed and going to work it out together. If you can maintain open lines of communication together, there's nothing that you cannot conquer together. The key here is that no matter what you face, KEEP TALKING!

Communication Styles

What was the communication style in your home? Make sure you take the time to understand how each of you learned to connect. It doesn't mean that it was automatically right or wrong; it's just that we need to understand where each other is coming from. For me, our family fostered a strong culture of sharing our thoughts (maybe too freely, haha) and emotions, so in marriage, I would want to go right after the conversations that mattered or confront the tension in the room, but Katie grew up with more of a "sweep it under the rug" approach to difficult conversations. So, much of the beginning of our marriage was me trying to figure out what Katie was actually feeling. There were a lot of "I'm Fine" statements, which, if you're new to marriage, "I'm fine" is code for "Everything is NOT fine." Now, even though my family did more communication, I also discovered I'm more instinctively a surface-level communicator, and my wife loves going deeper in connection. I am a much better friend, husband, father, and pastor because of learning from my wife to engage in relationships. We can all improve on connecting with each other and growing in our communication.

Here's an important note, have grace for each other's communication styles. Even though we needed to work on being more effective at communication, I find communication is also personality-driven. I am more of a verbal processor, and she wants to think about it and process it before we talk. As time has gone on, she's learned to deal with the conflicts in our marriage quickly, and I've learned to relax and allow her to have a moment to chill and process before we reconnect. So, fight the urge to label your spouse's communication as wrong because it's different from yours.

Create Space to Connect

One of the simple reasons communication breaks down is because we don't create the space for it. So while we may generally be talking daily, the communication that we're referring to is deeper communication about how each other is doing and where you're going together.

Connecting and communication doesn't always need a lot of time, but it does need to be intentional. Sometimes we need to talk it out. I've found that my wife often needs to talk out here day. Literally, from start to finish! Every last detail!! Ha! With the speed of life, we often pack our schedules and then don't have time to connect. Also, we noticed that a fun or romantic date can get messed with if you haven't been communicating well. Let me see if this scenario sounds familiar to you.

"You've been busy and haven't had a date in a month or two, and you finally get it on the calendar, and if you have kids, you coordinate the sitter and plan to head out on a date. But, then, one or both of you are a little crunchy (as my wife calls it) and maybe moody. So, conversations on the car ride to the restaurant aren't going well, maybe you're trying to figure out what's wrong with your wife or husband, but they are shut down or combative. So, you get into an argument and say something like, "Wow, we're finally on a date, and instead of enjoying it, you want to fight.

If that sounds at all familiar, then you're not alone. But why does this happen? Because you've not been connecting, and when you finally have a moment to connect, all the emotions finally come up but not usually in a good way.

Dates and Coffee Meetings

A couple of ways to help fix that is to be consistently dating. You don't need to be religiously tied to a date night, acting as if your marriage will fail if you don't have your weekly date night, but if it's not intentional and planned, it might often never happen. So, put it on the calendar and get consistent and intentional with dating your spouse.

Another great way to help your date nights be more fun and romantic is to create another space for communication that we'll call a coffee date or coffee meeting. Our friends and pastors, Dr. Matt and Mikala Hubbard, showed us this. It's a weekly touchpoint to review schedules, family, goals, budget, and other vital things. It's not a date, it's a meeting, but it also helps to add to your quality time. When you do this family meeting, you'll consistently deal with the important issues of life, and then your dates won't have to be a burst of emotions because you haven't talked about the budget or future or kids. These coffee meetings will also help your family continue to move forward with your goals and vision. Learn more about these at *samueldeuth.com/blog/marriage-meetings*

Choose to Go There!

If you want temporary peace, then you avoid difficult conversations, but if you desire long-term joy, love, and fulfillment in your marriage, then you need to choose to go there and deal with the difficult topics. Also, if you go there consistently, the emotions won't build up to an exploding point! It's important to know that it's ok and even good to argue or deal with conflicts in front of your kids. Many families try to never argue in front of their kids, so the kids never see their parents fight and resolve the conflict. We all have different ways of approaching our conflicts. But know that conflict can make you stronger and better if you choose to resolve it in unity. So, we will have some arguments in front of our kids to then also show them that we may have conflict, but conflict doesn't mean hate or anger or that we don't love each other. Conflict means we're working things out together. You don't want your kids to avoid conflict or disagreements, so model that in your marriage. Go there and face head-on the challenges that you're having.

One of the things that we can do that hurts our marriage is to ignore our feelings, emotions, or preferences to try and keep the peace. Or maybe if you're a very accommodating personality style, it can seem like you love your spouse by always going along with their preference, but if you continually ignore and shove down your own opinions, then they will boil over. It's okay to want to go to a different restaurant or have differing desires related to key areas like money or sex. Learn to express your perspective.

Secrets, Secrets, Hurt Someone

Don't have any secrets from your spouse. They should know everything. It may not always be fun, but they shouldn't be kept in the dark when you're going through something. This applies to significant addictions but also applies to things like being overwhelmed or insecure. Men, there are times when your guy friends are going to be able to help you process through something, and in the same way, ladies, your girlfriends are going to be able to support and provide perspective for you. But we don't keep secrets from each other. Secrets keep us and our relationship sick. I've heard it said, "You're only as sick as your secrets." On a similar note, don't share marriage struggles with your friends of the opposite sex. That can open up your marriage to unhealthy emotional attachments to someone outside of your marriage.

Therefore confess your sins to each other
and pray for each other so that you may be healed.
James 5:16 NIV

CHAPTER 9

SAFEGUARD #4
SERVING EACH OTHER

Do nothing out of selfish ambition or vain conceit. Rather, in humility value others above yourselves, not looking to your own interests but each of you to the interests of the others.
Philippians 2:3-4

Learn to place the proper value and honor on your spouse. This idea of value and honor was imprinted on me when I served at a marriage conference hosted by Dr. Gary Smalley, where he told the men to practice valuing and honoring their spouses when they walked into the room. Just as if a famous person walked into the room, and you kind of gasped with excitement and wonder. So, he said next time your spouse walks in the room, say, "(gasp), I can't believe I'm in the presence of greatness."

The level of honor and value you place on someone will determine how you serve them. Don't allow familiarity to move you from appreciating to taking your spouse for granted. Keep honoring your spouse in your words, heart, and actions, and watch how the emotions of love and thankfulness rise.

Focus on Serving Your Spouse First

In a world so focused on discarding relationships that no longer meet your needs, God's word has a different formula for fulfillment in relationships. In Philippians 2:3-4 we see God's word calling us to serve and care for others first. When we put the needs of others before our own, we'll see a healthier flow in our marriages. The most successful way this works is when both the husband and the wife focus on putting the needs of their spouse before their own. Both serving and focusing on fulfilling the needs of the other. But what if they don't put your needs first? Stay faithful to your covenant of marriage and keep putting their needs first, even when they neglect your needs. That's not the easy way or the world's way, but it is the God-honoring way and the way of true joy and love in relationships.

Learn to See the Gold in Each Other

Most of the time, when we're first married, it's easy to see and notice all of the things you love about your spouse, but after the honeymoon phase is over, we can seem to lose sight of those things and zero in on the negative. So, before you're married or after, take the time to learn and understand your husband/wife, and maybe even take different personality tests together to better learn how you both work. The Strengths Finder test is one I recommend. Another valuable book that's not an official personality assessment, but it is a tried and true test that reveals your spouse's love langue. It helps you both learn how you each like to give and receive love. It's called, The 5 Love Languages, by Gary Chapman. It highlights what he discovered are the primary ways we communicate love: Words of affirmation, Quality Time, Physical Touch, Acts of Service, and Gifts.

This a game changer in your relationship because we can get frustrated when we keep trying to love our spouse, but they don't seem to be feeling the love. For example, I have "Words of Affirmation" as a primary love language, I'll tell my wife all the time how amazing and beautiful she is and how much I love her, which is good, and I should keep doing that, but her primary love langue is Quality Time, which means that she's glad that I "said" I love her, but she wants me to show it by going out together on a date and by spending undistracted time with her. As you both discover these primary ways to love each other, it will help you better serve the needs and interests of your wife or husband. This can begin even in dating seasons, although just be careful with the physical touch in that season! Ha! Make your spouse's love langue the priority. Men, I think this is especially key for us to learn; understanding that learning your wife's love language is a part of the challenge and adventure of loving your wife well.

I often joke, but it's not really a joke; for women, this is a little easier. Usually, all men are primarily in the words of affirmation and physical touch realm. So, simply tell them they are amazing and have as much sex with them as possible! If you follow that plan, you essentially can stop reading this book. But, on the other hand, men need to read the whole book from cover to cover! With the simplicity of men in mind, I boiled down the five to just two. It may not be scientific, but I haven't found a man who disagrees yet! There are two new *super* love languages that I call Physical Time & Quality Touch! I know, cringe dad/preacher joke, but that pretty much sums up the love languages that I attempt to remind my wife of often.

No Time for Mind Reading

As much as you can avoid it, try not to make each other be a mind reader. Be clear and specific with what you want. Women, if you feel like your emotional tank is running dry, bring it up to your husband. Be honest with him. He wants to love you and meet your needs but may not always be clued in. Never be afraid of a strong hint! Part of serving each other comes from learning who your spouse really is to know how they operate or function and how they would need to be served. A note from my wife, "My husband knew I needed some quality time when I was going through something, and he stopped his work day and took me to coffee. But, I was also direct and told him I needed that quality time and the coffee date." When you've been married for a while, you can read each other's needs and emotional states, but as you grow into that, be as specific as you can be with each other. This will avoid the frustrations of unmet expectations.

Don't Attack the Differences: Celebrate Them!

A key lesson we learned early in our marriage from pastors Kevin and Sheila Gerald was to celebrate the differences and uniqueness of your spouse rather than attack it. As I quoted earlier, "Opposites attract, and then they attack." And if you think about it, it's so true, the unique part about your husband or wife that was fun or cute and different is now what can annoy you. Katie and I always joke about each other's "Pet peeves." She loved the way I was full of life and energetic, but now sometimes she's just like, "Why are you so loud?" I loved how focused, organized, and determined she was, and now I'm like, "Can you chill out!" In a recent sermon at Awaken Church on relationships, I joked that my wife loves everything about me; she only has a pet peeve about how I walk, talk, eat, sleep, and breathe! It's only funny because it's true. If we're not careful, those differences or pet peeves can start causing us to attack each other rather than just laughing and enjoying the differences in how God made each of us. You don't want your spouse to be the same as you! Sure, it might be easier to pick out a movie, dinner spot, or vacation destination, but that variance is what brings spice to your life!

Don't Use Your Love Language as a Weapon

A quick note on communication styles, while I love taking the personality tests and the five love languages tests, it's key that you use these resources as a way to understand your spouse and how to love them better, but don't use them as weapons to tell your spouse how they don't love you. Instead, use it to understand yourself better and how you best thrive and be able to articulate that to your husband or wife, but don't use it like, "If you don't give me words of affirmation, you're not getting quality time." Here's what I promise you: if you truly prioritize your spouse's needs, it will be amazing how your needs will get met.

Never-Ending Beautiful Discovery

Men, one of the things that the Holy Spirit taught me along the way in marriage is that God designed your wife to be un-conquerable. Because our instinct is to win, conquer and take territory, we can tend to get bored with things that we've figured out. But, if you've been married for very long, you know that just when you think you've got your wife all "figured out," then everything changes again! Initially, this reality frustrated me, but then God showed me the pure genius in His design to keep men on a constant journey of discovering their wives. So, don't think of understanding your wife as a specific finish line but a continuous journey of discovery. Even as I'm writing this chapter now, I'm about to go on our weekly coffee date/meeting, and I'm asking God to help me discover something new and great in my wife.

CHAPTER 10

SAFEGUARD #5
BEING IN COMMUNITY

Two are better than one, because they have a good return for their labor: If either of them falls down, one can help the other up.
Ecclesiastes 4:9-10 (NIV)

Much, and I do mean much, of the health of our marriage is due to the community we've planted our family in. In every geographic move our family made, a big driver of that was what atmosphere or soil I felt my wife and kids would thrive in. The "you and me against the world" vibe is great for romantic movie scenes but not great for real life. We need the strength of the community around us to receive the life, encouragement, and coaching our marriages need. When you buy seeds from a store, the seed packet will give you planting instructions. It tells you the best conditions for growing that particular flower or vegetable. In the same way, one of the planting instructions for our marriage would include being surrounded by healthy couples that model what you're looking for and provide wise counsel and accountability.

Make Church Central, Not Secondary

There may be three responses to this chapter's focus on connecting your family to a church community. First might be, "I'm not religious, and I'm just reading this to have a better marriage, but I don't need the church stuff." Second might be a bit indifferent to this because you occasionally attend a church, but you don't see how it will impact your marriage that much to prioritize church involvement. And the third group would be giving me a big AMEN because you know how key this is and have seen its value in your life. Of course, every couple that is a part of the church isn't automatically the ideal picture of a great marriage; I'm sure we all know someone who was a Christian and still found themselves in divorce court, but the truth is that while most of those people went into a church, they most likely didn't allow the church community into their lives.

The church community provides inspiration, accountability, and coaching.

We need to be able to call each other out and allow our spouse to challenge us, but often we need a third-party perspective that doesn't have the blind spots that we can often have in our relationships. Getting the benefits of church connection will require transparency and teachability. We often think that being a husband or wife will be natural or intuitive, but then we get a little way into marriage and realize how much effort and development it requires to be a great spouse. One of the shortcuts to being a better spouse is observing someone who is great at it. Being in close proximity to other married couples as they live out their marriage in front of you. It's one thing to take a course or read a book, but quite another thing to watch someone build a healthy marriage in real-time. Be especially mindful of this if you didn't have a great model of a Godly and healthy marriage in your own life. As Solomon reminded us, there's power in the collective.

Two are better than one, because they have a good return for their labor: If either of them falls down, one can help the other up. But pity anyone who falls and has no one to help them up. Also, if two lie down together, they will keep warm. But how can one keep warm alone? Though one

may be overpowered, two can defend themselves. A cord of three strands is not quickly broken.
Ecclesiastes 4:9-12 (NIV)

As it says in v12, the cord of three strands is not quickly broken, and together you can overpower what would come against you. You have an enemy that wants to mess with your marriage. But when you and your wife are in unity, and you have others around you that are adding to the strength of that rope, then you'll increase your ability to resist and guard against the enemy's attack.

His Kingdom First

Surrounding ourselves with the community of faith isn't just an accountability group; it is first and foremost about attaching our personal and family life to the cause and mission of Jesus!

But seek first the kingdom of God and his righteousness, and all these things will be added to you.
Matthew 6:33 ESV

We must put things in order; we must put first things first. If you want your life, relationships, work, and marriage to go well, then you have to honor God and seek his purpose over your individual or family goals. Having said that, you'll find that when you lay down your agenda and pick up heaven's agenda, then you'll end up getting both God's will and your desires fulfilled. But, if your marriage is all about you and your family's wealth or fulfillment, it will always feel hollow.

Community Makes Us Healthy

It's vital for women to have great women in their life to give healthy feedback, the same with men needing men to help them process. Find friends that are challenging you towards health. Here are four questions to ask yourself when considering who to take marriage advice from. You want to see the fruit of their life and marriage.

Do they love each other?
While commitment and longevity are important parts of the marriage commitment, you want to see that they aren't just "still together," but they're still in love.

Do they honor each other?
How do they treat each other? How do they speak to each other in front of the other and in private? I can see the evidence of a healthy marriage by how they interact in public.

Do they love their kids?
Parents who are just in a tolerating mode with their kids have a core deficiency that you don't want to replicate.

Is their life full and fun?
When a couple is still growing and going after goals and purpose in life, you can be more confident in their advice and counsel.

CHAPTER 11

SAFEGUARD #6
DEALING WITH THE PAST

"Forget the former things; do not dwell on the past. See, I am doing a new thing! Now it springs up; do you not perceive it? I am making a way in the wilderness and streams in the wasteland.
Isaiah 43:18-19 NIV

You may have heard it said that love is blind, and while it's great to be gracious to our spouse about their past, we must realize that showing grace doesn't mean ignoring. Too often, relationships get massively blindsided by hurts and dysfunction from our past that get unknowingly brought into our marriage. You may have heard people joke about going to Vegas, making bad decisions, and saying, "What happens in Vegas stays in Vegas." Now, that might be a catchy slogan, but anyone with a little common sense or experience knows that the bad decisions from Vegas always find their way out to the surface and, in the process, can destroy current relationships. While you may not have taken a regrettable Vegas-style hangover trip, we all have things in our past from our parents, friends, relatives, friends, or circumstances that have left us scarred, like abuse or tragedy. But, if we don't deal with it, we'll see it resurface later in marriage in a destructive way.

Do the Heart Work!

If you're reading this book before marriage, this would be a great time to discuss your past relationships and life experiences to see what might need to be healed and dealt with before you get married. I want to encourage you not to gloss over your past as if it's not a big deal; if it's not worked on, it will be a potential place of weakness and open access for the enemy to mess with your life. This is why we encourage all engaged couples or even those before engagement to attend pre-marriage classes with your church and do at least a few sessions with a marriage counselor. Those settings will allow challenges to surface that can be worked on. Some of it may be issues that can be dealt with quickly, and other past hurts may require a more in-depth healing process.

Brothers and sisters, I do not consider myself yet to have taken hold of it. But one thing I do: Forgetting what is behind and straining toward what is ahead, I press on toward the goal to win the prize for which God has called me heavenward in Christ Jesus.
Philippians 3:13-14 NIV

Wounds and Gaps

Some of the areas we need to work on aren't major traumas that one or both of you have had, but they might be more simple gaps in your training as a child. For example, you may not have experienced abuse, but if mom and dad didn't model a healthy marriage or model how to communicate well with each other, then those will be areas that need to be worked on. Also, if Dad or Mom wasn't around, that would be both a pain that needs to be healed and a practical training gap of not having a healthy example of what being a husband or wife should look like. In that case and in similar situations, you'll need to glean insight from another healthy source to be sure you start down the path of marriage with strength.

Even for me, as someone who had the privilege to grow up in a home with a dad and mom that loved each other and me, there were things once I got married that I started realizing were gaps. This doesn't speak poorly of my parents; they were and still are incredible, but my dad had a really dysfunctional home life growing up, and he overcame so much to be the amazing father he was, but he wasn't perfect. And so I got to learn from him all of the good and bad habits along the way, and I'll do my best to improve on it, but no doubt, I have some gaps and areas that I need to work on that will be passed along to my kids that they'll need to have help with as well. Our goal as parents should be to do our best to be a healthy and Godly example of marriage and parenting so that our children have to overcome as little as possible in their future. Still, there are always going to be some shortcomings, and we'll have to trust God's grace and goodness to see them through those gaps.

"Time doesn't heal all wounds; it just barriers them deeper.
You have to be intentional to deal and heal."
Dr. Brian Reiswig

Healing from Your History

I wish there were magic wands and quick fixes to erase some of the hurts and pains of our past, but the truth is the only way to work through it is to deal with it head-on. We can't ignore our dysfunctions; we must face them. An undealt with past hurt will become more and more of a hindrance to your marriage health. Healing can look different ways for different people. Sometimes it's simply that we need to learn something new that helps us overcome a deficiency from our past, but sometimes it takes us doing the work of forgiveness and counseling to overcome areas of trauma and neglect. Do the work of overcoming those pain points. Covering it up and sweeping it under the rug won't work. Go to God and ask for help and healing, go to your trusted circle of friends to get transparent and get healing, and when needed, reach out to a Christian counselor to help you walk through some of the core traumas or hang-ups in your life. Don't allow the stigma of counseling or coaching to keep you locked up.

Deliverance and Freedom

Some of you may not know that sometimes to truly get free from past hurts, it's going to take supernatural help. I love counselors, and my wife and I go from time to time to keep our marriage strong. But, sometimes, we're dealing with more than natural processing or past habit wiring; we may be facing a spiritual or demonic attack or oppression from the enemy due to hurt or trauma from the past. Physical abuse, sexual abuse, divorce, or abandonment can all be ways that the enemy tries to make his entrance into your life. If you need deliverance, go to a church that knows and believes in the Holy Spirit and operates in power so that they can help you break off that demonic attachment to your life. You also can take your God-given spiritual authority in Jesus' name to command the devil to leave your life! Then, be mindful not to allow new attacks of the enemy to stick to your life. One of the key ways we do this is forgiveness which we'll discuss in a later chapter.

"Above all else, guard your heart, for everything you do flows from it."
Proverbs 4:23 NIV

You're Not Meant to Carry Shame

One of the greatest killers of our relationships is shame and regret. Yes, you messed up and wish things would have been different, but that's where love and grace come in. The Bible reminds us that when we confess our sins to God, He is faithful to forgive them. You don't need to carry shame or guilt for your past. Jesus has forgiven you and sets you free.

So if the Son sets you free, you will be free indeed.
John 8:36 NIV

And if you've had to extend grace to your spouse for their failings, stop bringing up old sins and let them loose into freedom! The Bible reminds us that *real* LOVE keeps no record of wrongs.

CHAPTER 12

SAFEGUARD #7
HAVING FUN & CONNECTING

A cheerful heart is good medicine,
but a crushed spirit dries up the bones.
Proverbs 17:22 NIV

My wife is the fun instigator in our family! My default is to jump in on the fun that's planned, but if I'm honest, I'm not great at creating it in our family. I'm a work in progress in this area for sure. And while it may not be my default, having fun is a value I've learned to love and embrace. Joy and laughter are good medicine, which means they heal or keep something healthy in the first place. Laughter and joy in your marriage are a massive safeguard. You may have heard the phrase, those who play together stay together. And It's for these reasons mentioned in this verse. Being cheerful sends life into your marriage. When was the last time you had a good laugh together?

Notice the second half of that verse, a crushed spirit dries up the bones, and for this book's purposes, a crushed spirit dries up the marriage. When we've removed fun from our lives, we get dried up and are no longer able to nourish the bones of our marriage. Having a fun and full-of-life kind of marriage isn't an accident; it's intentional. We create a bond with those we're always having fun with. This is a powerful tool in marriage, friendships, co-workers, and our kids. Fun should be applied to all relationships, but be mindful that if you're all fun and play at work, but a lame lump of coal at home, then you'll start drying up what's at home and feeding the other areas of your life, which in extreme cases could lead to affairs and other emotional or sexual detachments and attachments.

Fun Requires Intentionality

We can easily see that what we focus on improves and grows. What we're intentional with always gets better. It's the same in our marriages; what you focus on will get healthier. And if you're the life of the party! That's great, keep it up, but don't let your desire to be fun or "busy" end up getting you on the other side of the ditch into distraction from truly having conversations and connecting. The key is that we create intentional space for play and fun. We look at our annual calendar and make sure that we have enough fun in our year. If we wait to take vacations or breaks until we feel we need them, we may not break until we actually see our family breaking down.

This was a key one for me to learn. This fully unlocked for me when our family joined Awaken Church. As we were getting connected, Pastor Jurgen and Leanne said, hey, we want you to go hang with the campus pastors at our north locations, Dr. Matt & Mikala Hubbard, because he said, "They know how to have fun." Initially, I thought it was a bit strange that they were sending me there to learn to have fun. He didn't say it was to learn to move in the power of the holy spirit, even though we did; he didn't say it was to learn to pray, even though we did. He said to learn to have fun. Many years since that moment, and a lot of fun vacations, river trips, dinner parties, and more, I learned to relax, enjoy life, and see the powerful impact that simply having fun brings to relationships. A note to introvert couples, you may not be a couple that needs to have ten activities a weekend, but all of us need to be intentional with having fun because one of the key benefits is that it opens up our communication and connection. Fun is different for everyone; you need to find your fun. No matter what it is—reading, hiking, concerts, etc.

Honor the Sabbath

This chapter feels like excessive use of the word fun, even for me, but let's look a little deeper, rest and rhythm aren't just about epic vacations. It's about trusting God and honoring how He designed us. He worked six days and then rested, and God calls us to do the same.

"Remember the Sabbath day by keeping it holy. Six days you shall labor and do all your work, but the seventh day is a sabbath to the Lord your God. On it you shall not do any work,"
Exodus 20:8-11 NIV

Invite God's blessing and rest into your life. Work hard, go all-in with all that God gives you and your family to do, but resist the urge to keep yourself so busy you can't slow down, trust and honor God, and just rest. There will always be another task you need to complete; there will always be a reason to spend a little more time on a work project. This is why resting and having fun is also about trust—trusting God's ability to do more with six days than you can with seven. Trusting that God is working with you in your marriage to fill in gaps and bring health and strength as you rest in Him.

CHAPTER 13

SAFEGUARD #8 THINKING & SPEAKING LIFE

Finally, brothers and sisters, whatever is true, whatever is noble, whatever is right, whatever is pure, whatever is lovely, whatever is admirable—if anything is excellent or praiseworthy—think about such things.
Philippians 4:8 NIV

This safeguard is one of the most practical, simple, and yet often the most difficult to do in marriage. The Bible says that just as a small rudder directs a massive ship, so our tongue or words direct our life. It's the same with our marriage. This is because our thoughts and words, no matter how small they may seem, will set the course of our relationships toward life or death. Our thoughts impact our emotions, and our words flow or overflow from our thoughts and feelings. If it feels like you're constantly speaking poorly to your spouse, that's usually because you're agitated or on edge emotionally with each other; which you can follow that trail of emotions back to the thoughts you've been thinking about your spouse.

On the one hand, this is frustrating because of the high levels of personal ownership and responsibility this puts on you and me. But, the good news also is that this means it's easy to fix. If the words I'm saying are not good, then I can simply begin to change my thoughts. The Bible gives us a clear word picture of the reality and power of our words.

The tongue has the power of life and death,
and those who love it will eat its fruit.
Proverbs 18:21(NIV)

It's critical to learn to truly see our words as injecting life or poison into our life, relationships, and marriage. We eat what we say. Our lives produce the same fruit as the seeds we're planting. So, likewise, the kind of words we use with our spouse will be the fruit we see in their life. So, how are your words doing? Do you like the fruit of them? What do you need to shift? How can you begin to speak life over your spouse?

Complaining Vs. Complimenting

Say what you want to see! This is a simple but massive key in our marriage. Instead of regurgitating what you see in your spouse that frustrates you, be intentional to speak about the good you see in them and say what you want to see, even if you don't quite see it yet. In marriage, we have the great vantage point of seeing areas where our spouse needs to change or adjust. If we each stay open to input, this is an excellent way that God will cause us to grow. But, when it becomes an overfocus on each other's flaws and complaining to them or about them, that's when you'll be hitting your head against the wall. You may be able to get your spouse to stop something by complaining enough, but you won't be able to get them to start something new other than with encouragement.

We can't force growth, but we can encourage it. A key to helping this growth is to focus on complimenting and encouraging rather than complaining. Of course, every healthy marriage will require calling out blind spots and areas of weakness that need to be addressed. But a healthy marriage majors way more on calling out the good!

What you focus on expands!

Focus on the good in each other. Whether it's easy right now or challenging to point out the good in the other, this is your moment to begin to shift the bulk of your thoughts and words in the direction of the good. If you keep looking for the bad, guess what? You'll keep finding it. And if you look for the good, guess what? You'll also start finding and seeing more of it. What we focus on will expand in every area of our marriage or any relationship. Speak life over each other. As humans made in the image of God, we have a creative power that we've been given to build up or tear down, add strength, or expose a weakness. Today, your spouse will most likely provide you with a chance to see the good and the bad in them, but make the decision to focus on the good!

Words Create Walls

Here's another thought on the power of our words. Your words will create walls. The question is, are they building walls to guard and protect your marriage, or are they creating walls between you and your spouse?

Those who guard their lips preserve their lives,
but those who speak rashly will come to ruin.
Proverbs 13:3

Just like God's Word created the world we live in, your words create the world that your marriage lives in. It's essential that we are intentional with the kinds of words we speak to our spouse. This is why we must be so specific with the words we choose. The Bible calls us to take every thought captive. Don't let any thought in that could harm your relationships or build walls between you.

We demolish arguments and every pretension that sets itself up against the knowledge of God, and we take captive every thought to make it obedient to Christ.
2 Corinthians 10:5

We must take captive wrong thoughts, and even more importantly, we want to work to be intentional about the right thoughts we're thinking about our spouse. Like Philippians 4:8 reminds us to think about what is good, I want to encourage you to maintain focus on the good in each other. As a practical step, take time to write down everything you love about your spouse and the reasons why you were attracted to them and said yes to marrying them. Then, if you're going through a time of frustration with each other or you notice anger or bitterness rising, stop and go read through your list and allow the rush of positive feelings and love to flood your heart again.

Thoughts Attract or Repel

Just like our words build walls, our thoughts and words can also attract or repel our spouse. No one goes into marriage with the idea of divorce or affairs, so why do some find themselves there? Very rarely would you find someone who accidentally had an affair. Now, we say that or use that terminology, like "we didn't want it" or "we just found ourselves in someone else's arms." But, if people are honest, affairs aren't an accident; they start with not challenging how we think about our spouse and how we're thinking about a man or woman that's outside of our marriage. The more our thoughts and attention is focused on someone other than our spouse, the more likely we are to create attachments to them and detach from our spouse. This is where the thought of "I just fell out of love" comes from. You didn't fall out of love, it's just that you stopped thinking about your spouse with affection and started thinking more about what agitates you and about the other person, and as a result, the feelings followed those thoughts.

Are your thoughts leading you towards or away from your spouse?

That's why I try not to entertain negative thoughts about my wife and why I'm committed to rejecting any romantic or sexual thought about another woman. To pretend those thoughts don't come is to ignore reality, but to think we can entertain them without hurting our relationships is pure stupidity. So be the guard of your heart and mind by focusing your thoughts on the good you see in your spouse! And in prophesying or speaking into the good you know is in them even if you don't fully see it yet!

Finally, brothers and sisters, whatever is true, whatever is noble, whatever is right, whatever is pure, whatever is lovely, whatever is admirable—if anything is excellent or praiseworthy—think about such things.
Philippians 4:8 NIV

Be Careful Who You Complain to

Now, this heading may seem confusing since we've been saying to not complain but focus on the positive; having said that, there are going to be those issues that you and your spouse are dealing with that you just don't seem to be getting resolution on. At that point, you have to choose how you will proceed. You can decide it's not a big deal and be okay with that friction, which I don't recommend. You can go and spout off and complain about it to anyone who will listen. Or you can intentionally choose to speak to someone or a small group of people that can help you.

What you don't want to do is, complain on social media and talk crap about your spouse to other friends who aren't helping you get healthy. On the other hand, you'll want to look for the right voices to express your frustrations to, which can help you. You'll want to look for people who love both you and your spouse. Don't share a negative thing about your spouse with a person who already wants you to leave them. You'll want to look for someone further down the track in marriage than you. If you've only been married a few years, find someone who's been married for 10 or 20 years. There's something powerful about perspective in marriage. You'll want to look for someone who is grounded in God's Word and gives you counsel from that position rather than from a purely personal or secular perspective. You'll want to look for someone or a couple that's willing to tell you the truth. You don't need someone to keep you in a victim state as a couple.

Don't Avoid Conflict

Now, focusing on the good doesn't mean avoiding conflict and only concentrating on surface-level issues. It's key that we don't withhold what needs to be said. Avoiding conflict is not a sign of life or health in your marriage. When there's conflict, it's a good sign that you're dealing with the things that matter. As time goes on, there should be growth and resolution from the initial conflicts, but issues will always need to be dealt with. Don't sweep them under the rug or get passive-aggressive about them. In love, face them head-on. When you face them, you can still face an issue with grace because you're going to be focusing on the good and the best in each other.

CHAPTER 14

SAFEGUARD #9 PLANNING FOR PURITY

Marriage is to be held in honor among all [that is, regarded as something of great value], and the marriage bed undefiled [by immorality or by any sexual sin]; for God will judge the sexually immoral and adulterous.
Hebrews 13:4 Amplified Bible

This word, PURITY, can pack many different meanings and carry a ton of emotions with it. So, let me set the groundwork for why we saw this as an essential safeguard. The definition of being "pure" is to be without contaminants. We want to keep our relationship and marriage pure from the things that can contaminate it. Just like a vehicle runs better on uncontaminated gasoline, our marriage will be smoother and stronger when we guard against things that can contaminate. So, what are the common things that can contaminate our marriage's purity?

- Pornography
- Sex outside of marriage
- Lust and unchecked thoughts

Before we go too far into this chapter, some of you may feel guilty already because you feel like you've already done things in dating or in your marriage that have messed with the fuel of your marriage, but let me encourage you that God can purify your life and your marriage again if you invite him into the mess. He will heal and restore your life.

Biblical Purity

For clarity purposes, when talking about purity, we're speaking specifically to the standards that God's Word sets out for us in relationships. Only He knows how our lives and relationships work best; He has the perfect formula for pure fuel. We don't want to define purity by phrases like, "Everyone else is doing it," or by the statement, "Well, at least I'm not as bad as other people." None of that matters; we must keep setting our standard of purity in our life before and during marriage based on the Biblical standard. Why does it matter? Because I have an intention and goal I'm building toward in my marriage, and I don't want anything to contaminate that plan. Our sex drive is God-given and incredible, but it's designed to drive us toward our wife or husband. So, when we use our sex drive to simply fulfill a temporary need or urge, we reduce the value of marriage and contaminate the marriage.

Purity Before Marriage

For those of you reading this book before marriage, you have a great opportunity to set up your future marriage by intentionally not contaminating the fuel of your life now. Before marriage, some of the key ways to keep yourself pure is to set up boundaries to support purity. This means that you're staying away from friend circles that don't care about biblical morality. It means that you're staying clear of strip clubs and similar scenes that you know will provide temptation that will take you out. It also means setting firm boundaries for what kind of content you allow into your heart through music and movies. It means that you're setting the right boundaries in dating. Often we resist boundaries because they feel like a bunch of rules, but instead of seeing them as a list of things you can't do, focus instead on choosing those boundaries because of what it will set up for you in your marriage.

To the men before marriage, we're challenging you to treat women with respect and purity for a few reasons. First, God cares how you treat women because they are His child; they aren't objects; they are the crown of His creation, and He places the highest value on them. Second, they are the daughter of another man that you must honor. And Finally, because they are the future wife of a man, It may be you, but if it's not, then you'll want to treat her with respect.

In dating, purity and abstinence matter because our goal in dating is to find a wife or husband, not to hook up. So, if our goal is to find love, romance, companionship, and a wife, then we want to create boundaries that get us in that direction. This is why you'll often hear pastors encourage Christians to only date Christians because they have the same agenda for dating and marriage. God's Word commands us not to unite ourselves to unbelievers.

Do not be yoked together with unbelievers.
For what do righteousness and wickedness have in common?
Or what fellowship can light have with darkness?
2 Corinthians 6:14 (NIV)

Purity in Marriage

We hear the word purity and assume it's for young people or just the dating scene, but walking in purity is just as crucial during marriage as it was before. It may look different in marriage because now having sex is no longer off limits, but keeping free from contaminants is key for relational longevity. Keeping your marriage pure will come from simple healthy boundaries and bigger-picture health conversations.

Six Ways to Support Purity In Marriage

1. Your thoughts.

Commit to thinking good about your spouse, like we've chatted, commit to only allowing yourself to think romantically or sexually about your wife or husband. When we entertain lust or attraction for someone other than our spouse, it has the ability to produce actions. Even if it never came to acting on those thoughts, just that affair of the mind can create a distance in your relationship. This is a good time not to get weird about the idea that a wrong thought may come to you about someone other than your spouse. Someone may catch your eye or make you feel a certain way, but that doesn't mean anything other than that, and it can be ended at that exact moment if you choose to guard your thoughts. Also, with this in mind, watch your inputs; what music, movies, and shows are you consuming? Are they promoting thoughts of marital faithfulness? For example, we love country music, but I limit listening to all the cheating and breakup songs. Why? Because I don't want to cheat or break up with my wife.

2. Your time

We're a fan of creating consistent date nights, but even if you don't have a weekly date on the books, the significant priority is that time is being spent together. Not just time in the bedroom, but generally prioritize having fun together and enjoying life. If you find that the only people you're laughing with and doing life with are people not in your home, you may create an open door for a breakdown in your marriage due to feeling more connected to that person at the office because of the time spent together. Get intentional about spending time together as a couple and as a family if you have kids.

3. Physical Boundaries

One of the things we commit to is avoiding as much as possible being alone with someone of the opposite sex that's not our spouse. We don't do lunch meetings or ride in a car alone with someone of the opposite sex. Do I do that because I don't think I can be trusted for 5 minutes with someone who's not my wife? No. I know I'd have no problem with it, but if you allow those moments to happen often, it can create room for something to happen that you didn't plan for. In an office situation where I need to meet with a female, I make sure that either there's a window that people can see in, or we just leave the door cracked so that it provides a layer of accountability. Again, this may seem a little prudish, but most of the time, we wait too long to set boundaries, and then it's too late because we've let thoughts and emotions build and run away.

4. Have same-gender best Friends

I'm concerned when couples have best friends other than their spouse that are the opposite sex. As a man, no woman should be my close friend and confidant other than my wife, and the same goes the other way around. Men, create close friends that are men you can go out with or have over. It's healthy. In the same way, women, get your girlfriends together and build those close friends. We need good friends in our lives, but if you're a woman, the only male best friend you need is your husband, and same with men, your wife is and must remain the main female voice in your life, above other others and as a note that includes your mother.

5. Eliminate Pornography

Porn isn't innocent and does negatively impact our marriages. Some have thought that watching porn together would somehow help the couple's sex life, but that will only serve to defile it. If you feel your sex life is getting boring, talk with a counselor or some trusted friends, but introducing porn will only create greater dissatisfaction. Also, if one or both of you are consuming porn on your own, that will rob from your marital intimacy. Porn becomes a poor substitute for sexual intimacy and diminishes your sexual drive toward your spouse. Having said that, pornography addictions can be common. So, don't live in shame and guilt; confess it and get help to break free. A note to the wives, if you find out your husband is struggling with a pornography addiction, this can be very hurtful in how it feels to you, and yes, it is robbing from your marriage. But, I want to encourage you that pornography addictions are not typically a sign that your husband doesn't love you or isn't interested in you; it is just a temptation and lust that's out of control and unsubmitted. It needs to be dealt with, and it can be fully overcome, but don't allow the enemy to get you thinking that your husband doesn't love you or an even greater lie that you aren't loved or valuable or desirable to your husband. It's right to take a firm stand that you are not okay with any pornography in your home and marriage, but also express your love to your husband and encourage him to open up to the right men in his life that can help him get freedom and victory. Knowing you're with him in his battle will be incredibly helpful.

6. Stay Away From Temptations

Be honest about your areas of weakness and temptation that you know will likely lead you toward sin. Whether that's social media, a movie streaming service, a bar, or a club, be mindful of the atmospheres you put yourself in.

At the window of my house I looked down through the lattice. I saw among the simple, I noticed among the young men, a youth who had no sense. He was going down the street near her corner, walking along in the direction of her house at twilight, as the day was fading, as the dark of night set in.
Proverbs 7:6-9 NIV

Four Drivers of Purity

As I mentioned, it's not just about protective boundaries that keep marriage pure; it's more about the intentional things we do to build a healthy marriage that is a safeguard to keeping us pure. So, that's the focus of this whole book, but I'll also mention a few big things that keep purity in marriage.

1. A desire to Honor God

The Bible says that the fear of the Lord is the beginning of wisdom. So, our desire for purity in our personal lives and in our marriage begins with our drive to please and honor God. We are children of God, which means that our heavenly Father is very interested in how you treat His son or daughter in your care. We will give an account to God for how we treat or mistreat each other.

2. A true love for our spouse

When you love them and keep those thoughts and passions for them, you'll want to keep living in a way that honors them. And when you love your spouse well, it will keep enhancing their affection for you. So what could you do to keep stoking the fires of romance? Plan more little getaways, date nights, and vacations. Be intentional with prioritizing sexual intimacy. Don't leave each other sexually starved.

3. Dream Together

I will talk about this more later, but if there's no dream and vision as a couple, it can be easy to become roommates going through the motions rather than having a mission that's uniting you together. Having a mountain to climb or a giant to conquer will keep you teaming up together towards purpose. This also goes back to the chapter about keeping God as the central priority.

4. Have Fun Together

Try things like axe throwing or go-karting, anything to switch it up and have fun! Whether it's major vacations or simple coffee dates, be intentional to keep laughing together! It's a healing and bonding experience.

Restoration is Possible

Trust is the bedrock of our relationships. Infidelity destroys that trust. If there has been a breach in your relationship, it doesn't have to mean it's over. It won't be easy and will require massive transparency, accountability, and lots of grace. But, with God's help, you can see a healthy and thriving marriage again! I've seen God do it over and over again in marriages from people in church! I was just talking to a couple this week who was married, got divorced, then had encounters with God that led them to work through rebuilding trust, and they got re-married again! Now they're thriving and setting an incredible example of grace, forgiveness, and God's restoration power!

CHAPTER 15

SAFEGUARD #10
HAVING GREAT SEX

May your fountain be blessed, and may you rejoice in the wife of your youth. A loving doe, a graceful deer— may her breasts satisfy you always, may you ever be intoxicated with her love.
Proverbs 5:18-19 NIV

Strong and healthy marriages have a great sex life. I'm not saying that their sex life is perfect or always a 10 out of 10, but it's a consistent and mutually satisfying part of their marriage, or at least that's the direction it's progressing. Sex functionally is for fulfilling the mandate on humanity to increase and multiply and fill the earth with people. But, in God's goodness, he made the process a beautiful bonding and intimate time as well as a wildly fun and euphoric experience. Sex between a husband and wife is a powerful part of the longevity of the marriage. I've heard it said that intimacy is a part of the glue that holds the marriage together, and we agree with that wholeheartedly.

Biblical Stance On Sex

Sex is God's idea and is biblically celebrated and honored. Sometimes, however, there's a perceived idea that sex is taboo in church or that great sex is really for the wild non-Christians and that followers of Jesus need to strip away all the passion and pleasure side of sex. But, the fact that the Bible has an entire book dedicated to romance should be a great indicator of the heart and intention of God. Sex is not just a mundane act for making babies but is also designed for mutual fulfillment and enjoyment.

Movie Sex Isn't Real Life

Sometimes we put a lot of pressure on sex. We want it to look like or be like some movie or even can unintentionally compare our spouse to previous sexual partners or pornography. But, part of the beauty of marriage is a lifelong journey of discovering what your spouse loves or doesn't want in bed. That exploration process also builds emotional intimacy. And don't freak out if, at the time of reading this book, your sex life isn't looking good. My wife and I have had different seasons of sexual passion. Over two decades of marriage, we've had passionate seasons, going thru the motions seasons, roommate seasons, and everywhere in between. The key is to keep working on your intimacy, don't settle in any season.

Boundaries In Sex

As we're exploring and growing together sexually, it's great to try new things to keep things fun, but what's too far, or what should be off-limits? I have some general guidelines around sex that I recommend, but much of the sexual boundaries in marriage are up for your personal interpretation and comfortability. If you both are comfortable with it, I'd say enjoy freedom in the bedroom! Have fun and try new things if that helps you keep your passion alive. Get other resources that give ideas on how to spice up the bedroom. But, the most important thing is to communicate how you're each feeling about it before you try something new. Don't assume your spouse is enjoying the new thing you're trying either; simply ask if they like it. Ask if they are enjoying how it feels. Don't get offended if they don't—keep exploring each other until you find the pleasure points for each other.

Now, as for our personal recommendations to keep away from. We discourage sexual activity that isn't natural or how God indented your body to function. For example, anal sex is not natural or how God intended your body to work, and it isn't healthy for your body. Also, stay away from things that denigrate your spouse or things that are trying to replicate pornographic sex acts you've seen or heard of. If you try to bring in sex practices from an empty culture, you'll find that you're inviting emptiness into your marriage.

Don't Use Sex As A Weapon

Sometimes in marriage, if there's frustration or friction, one or the other can attempt to withhold sex as a power move of control. However, sex is not to be used in this way. That's damaging to the health and strength of your bond as a couple. Intentionally using sex in that way is like using the divorce word as the trump card in an argument.

But since sexual immorality is occurring, each man should have sexual relations with his own wife, and each woman with her own husband. The husband should fulfill his marital duty to his wife, and likewise the wife to her husband. The wife does not have authority over her own body but yields it to her husband. In the same way, the husband does not have authority over his own body but yields it to his wife. Do not deprive each other except perhaps by mutual consent and for a time, so that you may devote yourselves to prayer. Then come together again so that Satan will not tempt you because of your lack of self-control.
1 Corinthians 7:2-5

Unfulfilled sexual needs in your spouse can leave an open door for the devil to enter and create division in your marriage. Are there going to be times when you just aren't feeling it, aren't in the mood, maybe on your time of the month, or are feeling sick? Yes, of course, and there needs to be grace for each other in those moments, but if that becomes the rule rather than the exception and sex becomes rare, this will threaten your marriage's strength. Now, should your spouse be able to withstand and stay away from other forms of sexual fulfillment even if you deny them? Yes, but why would you want to make it that hard for them, and why would you want to open the door for infidelity in your relationships just because you're not feeling like having sex? Men usually have a stronger sex drive. With that in mind, a dry season in your marriage is not a license to find fulfillment in other ways. Women, make it a goal to keep your husband sexually satisfied.

Warning Lights

Sexual tensions are common and are great warning lights on the dashboard of your marriage. One of the things I've learned over the life of our marriage is that when my wife has been closed off to me sexually, it's usually an indicator that something in our marriage is off track or disconnected.

Key Things That Impact Sexual Intimacy:

1. Physical Health. Out of shape or physical issues.
2. Mental Pressure. Challenges of life and the schedule. Parent life. Kids can be a massive drain on your energy.
3. Finances. One of the most significant battles that cause a woman to shut down is being overwhelmed by where you are financially.
4. Lack of quality time or deficiency in your spouse's specific love language. If you haven't been having fun and connecting, it's going to create that resistance to you sexually.

Love Your Wife To Unlock Her

Men, as I noted earlier, God strategically designed your wife as an unconquerable part of your life. In the sense that we as men are always looking to fight and win and conquer and then move on to the next conquest, but in the case of your wife, what you felt like opened her up and turned her on this month, week, or yesterday isn't guaranteed to work today. This used to frustrate me until I realized this was God's design to keep me chasing and figuring out my wife. The challenge is when we, as men, assume we shouldn't have to keep fighting for our wife and then give up when it becomes a challenge and opt to find our fulfillment sexually somewhere else. But that will be the death of your marriage. So, keep chasing and pursuing your wife!

Unlocking or opening up sexual intimacy is less about sex drive and more about the other areas of your life. In some of our dry seasons sexually, I would usually want to resort to asking if there's some medical problem in my wife, but any time there's been a lack of interest sexually, it's always been resolved through maturing our relationship to better serve each other. My wife wanted me to note that security has been the most crucial key to unlocking her sexually. If she doesn't feel secure and safe and honored and made time for, if security and quality time isn't happening, then it affects her sex drive and makes most women uninterested. The biggest game changer in your marriage's sex life has less to do with sex and a lot more to do with the world you're creating for her to live in.

Final Encouragement

Men, keep working on unlocking your wife like a fun puzzle to solve rather than an issue to fix. Make your wife's sexual pleasure the goal. Women, fight to overcome those barriers that may block your sex drive. Don't make him have to earn it all the time but make it your gift to give. Make fulfilling your husband sexually your goal. Trust us, when you keep serving each other, you can have a sex life that continues to build in emotional and sexual intimacy and passion.

CHAPTER 16

SAFEGUARD #11 FORGIVING...AGAIN

Be kind and compassionate to one another, forgiving each other, just as in Christ God forgave you.
Ephesians 4:32 NIV

This is going to be a big one. Every healthy marriage that goes the distance has learned how to create a culture of grace and forgiveness in their home. To think that we'd be able to go through our marriage without needing to forgive would be very naïve; I'm sure no one reading this book would assume that. Having said that, most of the time, we're not truly ready for the lifestyle of forgiveness needed in healthy relationships, specifically in marriage. The challenge with unforgiveness is that its subtle, little offenses build up and harm us over time. Before you know it, there's a forest of pain blocking the sunlight that used to be giving your marriage life. Unforgiveness and resentment will choke out the life in your marriage. For Katie and I, we had to really work on a lot of this at the beginning of our marriage. For my wife, acknowledging her faults and asking for forgiveness wasn't instinctive to how she was raised. It was a learning process to engage both her and my issues with grace. It was less about her being so focused on wanting to attack my issues as it was more of an insecurity about getting honest and transparent. Her default was to see her own issues as a reason that I would reject her. Trust had to be built so she could be vulnerable with her issues, knowing that I would meet them with grace and, in the same way, she was learning to extend grace towards my issues. I also had to learn how to extend grace when an expectation went unfulfilled as we were learning to communicate better and connect.

The Source of Forgiveness

If you're not a follower of Jesus, it will be more challenging to walk out grace and forgiveness for your spouse. Why do I say that? Because Jesus did something on the cross for us that was unthinkable. The Bible says that while we were still sinners, he died for us. Before we deserved it and before we earned it, God extended forgiveness and mercy to us. It's a no strings attached type of grace, and he calls us to extend the same grace to each other. Because God has forgiven you, there's nothing anyone could do to you that you shouldn't forgive.

Forgiveness doesn't mean that we ignore realities. For example, suppose you're dealing with addictions, you may extend grace, but it's wise to require them to prove by their actions that they've changed before you trust them again. And there are times, unfortunately, for safety, one spouse may need to leave the marriage. But, most of the time, all the challenges our marriage comes against can be helped and healed by forgiveness. So if you have a hard time letting go of something your husband or wife did, then begin by going to Jesus and asking for strength and a reminder of his grace toward you.

Love is patient, love is kind. It does not envy, it does not boast, it is not proud. It does not dishonor others, it is not self-seeking, it is not easily angered, it keeps no record of wrongs. Love does not delight in evil but rejoices with the truth. It always protects, always trusts, always hopes, always perseveres.
1 Corinthians 13:4-7

Forgiveness Is a Choice

A foundational phrase in marriage is that love is a choice, and equally is that forgiveness is a choice. Why? Because you're not going to always feel love and grace towards your spouse, but we must still choose to forgive. God's word calls us to keep no record of wrongs. To extend unearned grace and forgiveness. If your spouse has caused you pain in your marriage, in a big or small way, decide to extend grace and not bring up the past. With God's help, forgive right away and every time.

Love is patient, love is kind. It does not envy, it does not boast, it is not proud. It does not dishonor others, it is not self-seeking, it is not easily angered, it keeps no record of wrongs. Love does not delight in evil but rejoices with the truth. It always protects, always trusts, always hopes, always perseveres.
1 Corinthians 13:4-7 NIV

Forgiveness Covers and Restores

The Bible says that love covers! It's so true. It's incredible how God's love extended from you to your spouse can restore and bring things back to life. So don't wait until you think the other deserves your forgiveness; choose today to be the one who shows grace, mercy, and the heart of God to your spouse. Being quick to forgive will keep your marriage light and full of life!

Above all, love each other deeply, because love covers over a multitude of sins.
1 Peter 4:8 NIV

CHAPTER 17

SAFEGUARD #12 BUILDING YOUR FAMILY VISION, MISSION, & PURPOSE

The Lord had said to Abram, "Go from your country, your people and your father's household to the land I will show you
Genesis 12:1 NIV

In any area of business or ministry I've been a part of or in any church I've coached, one of the consistent things we have to focus on is vision. If there's no vision for growth and expansion, then the church or business will not advance. Our homes are similar, and men, we're called to lead the way in this. Do you have a vision for your family, your marriage, your kids, your finances, your calling, or your career? Let's look at the essentials of vision, purpose, and mission to see how they safeguard our marriage.

Vision And Purpose

Where there is no vision [no revelation of God and His word], the people are unrestrained; But happy and blessed is he who keeps the law God].
Proverbs 29:18 Amplified Bible

Vision and Purpose are key health factors in marriage and family. Purpose puts a demand on our lives in all areas, mentally, physically, emotionally, and spiritually. When I'm saying demand, I'm not saying that in a bad sense. The demand calls out the best in us. The demand keeps us alive and on track. The vision pulls us out of a mundane life and into a beautiful and full life. Throughout the Bible, God calls individuals or families to step up and out into the unknown, and usually into the uncomfortable. God would give them a word or a call, and that would drive their life. When we leave the path and purpose of God, that's when we start declining. King David became an example of this when the bible says in 2 Samuel that when it was the time for Kings to go out to war, David stayed home. And when he did, that's when all hell broke loose in his life. Lack of purpose led him towards infidelity and murder. Vision keeps the wheels on your life. Purpose gives you drive.

There are many excellent books and resources on vision that you'll want to dive into. But for the purpose of this book, I'll give us a working definition of vision, purpose, and mission.

Vision is where we're going
Purpose is why we're doing it
Mission is who we're doing it for

Live With Purpose

I'm going to chat more about clarifying vision, but what drives your vision is purpose. Purpose ultimately comes as we link our personal and family vision to the house of God and His purpose. Part of why a marriage can feel average is because many marriages aren't driven by purpose and mission. Everything in life is better and enhanced when we live out of our purpose and values. Even greater when the purpose is beyond ourselves and focused on Kingdom-purpose. Living with purpose creates an alignment in your life and family that nothing else can do.

But seek first his kingdom and his righteousness,
and all these things will be given to you as well.
Matthew 6:33 NIV

Put the plan and purpose of God first in all you do. This means that you pray and ask for direction on specific things he wants you to do, but even more than that, it means that in all that you do, you're thinking about how you can advance and establish His Kingdom on Earth. Things that keep you and your marriage on purpose are identifying key none negotiables that you will focus on. We took time to shape vision and values statements that capture what we feel God has for us. I'll list out the values that keep us on purpose. Let these encourage and inspire you as you shape your values.

Deuth Family Values:
Multiplication (Growth)
Kindness (Honor)
Peace (Trust)
Rhythm (Generosity)
Commitment (Integrity)
Fun (Life)

Live With Vision

Purpose in your life is key, and vision clarifies you so that you can move forward! It helps you individually and as a family. Habakkuk says to write the vision and make it plain so you can run with it. Vision causes us to be able to run with the mission and purpose that God has for us.

Then the Lord answered me and said, "Write the vision And engrave it plainly on [clay] tablets So that the one who reads it will run.
Habakkuk 2:2 Amplified Bible

My pastor, Jurgen Matthesius, relayed a conversation that he and Pastor Phil Pringle had about staying focused and pure as a man in ministry, and I think it applies to all of us. Ps Phil said, "It's simple, spend your own money, sleep with your own wife, and keep building buildings. I love this! The first two things are pretty obvious. But that third one on building buildings is unique. Why would he say that? Because the building project or vision keeps us focused and moving forward. Staying on-mission keeps us from the wrong things by focusing us on all the right things. So what "building" or vision do you need to get to work on? What vision is God calling you to fulfill as a family?

Keep Your Marriage Centered In Christ

I've already said this many times, don't make following Jesus an optional thing as a family but the primary thing that all of life flows out of. Commit all of your ways to Him. Live devoted to following Jesus and watch every area of your marriage thrive over time.

But if serving the Lord seems undesirable to you, then choose for yourselves this day whom you will serve, whether the gods your ancestors served beyond the Euphrates, or the gods of the Amorites, in whose land you are living. But as for me and my household, we will serve the Lord."
Joshua 24:15 NIV

CHAPTER 18

FINAL ENCOURAGEMENT

Therefore, what God has united and joined together,
man must not separate [by divorce]."
Mark 10:9 Amplified Bible

We're praying this book was an encouragement, maybe some comic relief, and that you're left with some good practical ways to safeguard and build a healthy and passionate marriage. Don't be discouraged or overwhelmed with needing to get it all right and having it all worked out; continue to grow little by little. I'll leave you now with the simple encouragements that I share with couples on their wedding day:

Have fun, and laugh with each other, not at each other. Forgive often and quickly. Keep Jesus at the center of your marriage. Have as much sex as you can handle. Never use the word divorce. Pull the gold out of each other. And last, don't quit! Stay faithful until death do you part!

CHAPTER 19

BIBLICAL DATING GUIDE

He who finds a wife finds what is good
and receives favor from the Lord.
Proverbs 18:22 NIV

If you're single or dating and you jumped right to this section, welcome! Marriage is God's design, and it will unlock some of God's greatest treasures in life! In this Biblical dating guide, we're going to share several Biblical dating mindsets and safeguards that will help you find the love of your life and set you up for an incredible marriage that lasts a lifetime! This is a Biblical dating guide because only God and His Word have the principles that will produce life. We don't want to mirror or be conformed to the pattern of this world. Some of the concepts in this guide may be foreign to you if you've not been raised to set The Bible as the foundation for your life and relationships, but I encourage you to trust God's Word, and you'll see it produce health and strength.

Trust in the Lord with all your heart and lean not on your
own understanding; in all your ways submit to him,
and he will make your paths straight.
Proverbs 3:5-6 NIV

5 Biblical Dating Mindsets

1. God Created Marriage

God created me for relationships and to enjoy the intimacy of marriage. Continue to go to God's word for relationship wisdom because He is the author of friendship, relationships, and marriage. God says marriage is between a man and a woman. No other combination is blessed or endorsed by God.

The Lord God said, "It is not good for the man to be alone.
I will make a helper suitable for him."
Genesis 2:18 NIV

2. Commitment is a Good Thing

Committing to marriage is a good thing! You don't need to keep your options open; you need to find that woman or man and give yourself and your future fully to them for your whole life.

He who finds a wife finds what is good
and receives favor from the Lord.
Proverbs 18:22 NIV

3. Date Likeminded Believers

Because marriage is beautiful, intimate, and forever, I am looking to share that with someone who shares my same values of faith in Jesus. Avoid missionary dating, which is dating someone who isn't a Christian, hoping that they become a Christian. Consider the qualities that you're looking for in a future spouse, beginning with Biblical essentials and then your personal preferences of what is attractive to you. Don't settle for just anyone, be specific about who you date.

Do not be yoked together with unbelievers. For what do
righteousness and wickedness have in common?
Or what fellowship can light have with darkness?
2 Corinthians 6:14 NIV

4. Date with Marriage in Mind

The primary purpose of dating is to find a wife or husband. If you're just looking for more friends, then just stay friends. Romantic relationships should be progressing forward, so if you don't see the potential of marrying that person, don't use them to temporarily fill a void of loneliness.

That is why a man leaves his father and mother and is united to his wife, and they become one flesh.
Genesis 2:24 NIV

5. Sex is for Marriage

I'm reserving my full self, including my sexual purity, exclusively for my spouse. I won't be perfect, but by God's grace, I want to be as healthy and whole mentally, emotionally, and physically going into my marriage. I see my sex drive as God-given but as designed only for the power of marriage. I don't date to have sex; I date to lead me to my future spouse.

Marriage is to be held in honor among all [that is, regarded as something of great value], and the marriage bed undefiled [by immorality or by any sexual sin]; for God will judge the sexually immoral and adulterous.
Hebrews 13:4 Amplified Bible

With those Biblical mindsets in place, here are seven dating guardrails or safeguards to best set up your dating relationship to honor God and each other. If you apply these safeguards, it will help you date well and find out if the person you're dating is or isn't the one. *Be Friends First, if Possible;* Getting to know them before dating them can be a huge advantage. That way, you see how they really are rather than the polished-up version of them. Having said that, if that isn't an option, then just be sure to take time to focus on getting to know them before moving the relationship forward romantically.

7 Dating Safeguards

1. Date with Your Eyes Wide Open

When you begin to date, look for Godly character qualities if you haven't already seen them during friendship. And yes, physical attraction is essential! That should be obvious, but some Christian circles might downplay the importance of being sexually/physically attracted, while Godly character is the most important; we all have unique qualities we're attracted to; you should go after what you like but with a Biblical filter. Also, don't downplay the negative issues that come up. Whatever you ignore in dating will become a bigger issue in marriage. Ask questions and confront those areas of concern.

Charm is deceptive, and beauty is fleeting; but a woman who fears the Lord is to be praised.
Proverbs 31:30 NIV

2. Make Jesus the Center of Your Relationship

If the girl or guy you're pursuing isn't interested in growing their relationship with Jesus and isn't actively a part of a church community, then you may want to consider someone else. You don't want to have to drag your spouse to church in the future or fight over whether or not to teach your kids the Bible. When your relationship is connected to a growing church, it will also keep your relationships growing and healthy!

Do not be yoked together with unbelievers. For what do righteousness and wickedness have in common? Or what fellowship can light have with darkness?
2 Corinthians 6:14 NIV

3. Save Sexual Intimacy for Marriage (and anything close to that)

Before dating, make sure that you both chat about the boundaries you're committing to keeping when it comes to physical displays of affection. This isn't about creating weird or unrealistic rules, but it's about Biblical guardrails. Saving your sexual purity until marriage may not be common in today's culture, but it's very doable if you're intentional. How far is too far in dating? This can often be the question, but it shouldn't be your focus. Technically, the answer is simple; you can go until the line of sin. But it's hard to get that close to sin without sinning. So, I'd suggest staying further away from sin. And when it comes to specifics before marriage, any level of sexual activity, whether traditional sex or oral sex or anything with the word sex in it, would be too far. Also, excessive kissing, cuddling, and caressing can lead you down that path if you're not careful. You'll want to plan ahead and set healthy boundaries that support purity.

Flee from sexual immorality. All other sins a person commits are outside the body, but whoever sins sexually, sins against their own body. Do you not know that your bodies are temples of the Holy Spirit, who is in you, whom you have received from God? You are not your own; you were bought at a price. Therefore honor God with your bodies.
1 Corinthians 6:18-20 NIV

4. Surround Yourself with Healthy Friends and Mentors

Have good people to give you perspective. Love gives us blind spots, so we need others to speak into our lives and into our dating to be sure we choose the right spouse. A great practice is to vet out a potential man or woman you're interested in with your parents, friends, and leaders and with people who would know that person well. Staying open to input all through your dating relationship is key. Don't be defensive if they see something unhealthy.

Walk with the wise and become wise,
for a companion of fools suffers harm.
Proverbs 13:20 NIV

5. Don't Drag It Out...Put a Ring on it!

Get engaged or turn them loose. Don't play house or avoid commitment. Your relationship will never be what it can be and what it's called to be until you commit. Now how long should you date for? Although, honestly, there's no specific length of time; if you love them and can't see your life without them, and you're getting the green lights from the family and friends around you, then why wait? Propose and take your relationship to the next level!

6. Stay Mission Focused

One of the common mistakes that people make is to leave the pathway they are on to go chase the girl or guy that they are interested in. People abandon calling, friend groups, cities, church communities, and more for the sake of trying to chase the individual. But, this doesn't usually work out; the better approach is to stay on mission. That passion and focus that you have is a key part of what makes you attractive to them in the first place. Women, look for a man who is busy and consumed with their passions, work, and calling. You don't want a man with too much time on their hands. Men, look for a woman that is passionate about their purpose, which should include being a wife and mother. Men, you don't leave your calling to chase the girl. You chase your calling and invite the woman to join you on your mission.

7. Have fun and enjoy life together

While it can feel like a lot of pressure to find your future husband or wife, it's also key that you don't take it too seriously in the sense that a big part of how your marriage will last is that you learn to have fun with your spouse and live life to its fullest! Although you're building toward marriage, and that's a big deal, the best way to arrive at the altar is laughing and full of great memories during your dating and engagement season.

How to Break Up Gracefully, if Needed

One of the values of following the above practices is that if the person you're currently dating isn't the right one for you, when you break up, you'll have a lot less physical and emotional trauma to deal with. Yes, a breakup when you love someone is always difficult, but if you remain sexually pure, it's much easier to break up if you need to. Be kind to the other person in a breakup. Don't feel the need to smear anyone through the mud in a breakup. Instead, treat them with respect, like you'd want someone to treat you. And if you do need to break up, don't do it over txt or dm's, be respectful enough to speak in person.

A Note to the Men

I know this might seem obvious, but it's key that you, as a single man, understand you have the primary role in being intentional to "Find" your wife. Don't sit around waiting and hoping that she will come along. Be intentional about pursuing the woman that you could see yourself marrying. You won't know if she'll go out with you unless you get some courage and ask her out on a date! Make the first move and begin leading the relationship from the start. You aren't designed to do life alone!

He who finds a wife finds what is good
and receives favor from the Lord.
Proverbs 18:22 NIV

What Should You Look for in a Spouse?

Below we've listed 10 qualities to look for in a man or woman you'd want to date and marry. The person you're dating or interested in asking out may not have 100% of the qualities listed below, but you'll want them to have most of them or at least know they are connected to the right people helping them develop in that direction. Also, if you discover the person you're considering dating doesn't have one of the important items, before you immediately write them off, go to your trusted parents, pastors, or mentors to make sure you're not making a big deal out of something that's not a big deal. Or maybe they'll help you see something as more important than you were thinking. Finally, as you look over the lists below for men and women, you may feel more or less passionate about something we've listed. This is an example list that you may want to add or adjust based on what you're looking for.

The main reason to have a list like this is to make sure that you don't just jump into a relationship out of emotions and attraction without stepping back and asking yourself if they match up with the kind of person you want to marry.

Biblical Qualities to Look for in a Man

1. He Loves God and leads the way in your commitment to following Jesus, going to church, and serving the purposes of God with your lives. Grace needs to be applied here since we're all on a journey of learning to lead our families spiritually; you just don't want to be dragging your boyfriend to church.
2. Has a strong work ethic. You don't want a lazy dreamer who talks big but never does anything.
3. He loves his family or, at minimum, honors them. This is important and gives you a window into how he'll eventually treat you.
4. He lives in obedience to the Bible, not in response to culture.
5. Gives his tithes and offerings at church. You don't want to marry someone who robs God.
6. Levels of self-control. None of us are perfect, but you'll look to be sure there are no significant addictions or habits that could take him out, like drunkenness, excessive gambling, drugs, pornography, etc.

7. A man of integrity. You're looking for a man of his word who follows through on commitments.
8. You're looking at his friends. This is a big one because we tend to attract who we really are. So, it doesn't mean that if he has lame/weird friends, he is, but there's a stronger chance, so you just need to take the time to vet him out.
9. Look for a good reputation with those in authority and peer groups. How do others talk about him?
10. You're looking for a man that respects your femininity and purity. So keep your distance from any guys who want to cross the sex boundary before marriage.

Biblical Qualities to Look for in a Woman

1. She loves God and has a personal relationship with Jesus. She may still be growing in her faith, but you don't want to have to drag her to church every week.
2. She sees her value as a princess/daughter of God but isn't conceited and full of herself.
3. She loves her family or, at minimum, honors her family. This is important and gives you a window into how she'll eventually treat you.
4. She lives in obedience to the Bible, not in response to culture.
5. Gives her tithes and offerings at church. You don't want to marry a woman who robs God.
6. Levels of self-control. None of us are perfect, but you'll look to be sure there are no major addictions or habits that could take her out. Like, drunkenness, gossiping, drugs, pornography, etc.
7. A woman of integrity. You're looking for a woman who keeps her word and follows through on commitments.

8. You're looking at her friends. This is a big one because we tend to attract who we really are. So, it doesn't mean that if she has lame/weird friends that, she is lame, but there's a stronger chance, so you need to take the time to vet her out.
9. She has a good reputation with those in authority and peer groups. How do others see her?
10. You're looking for a woman that respects you and your purity. Keep your distance from any woman who dresses to seduce you or who uses sex to lure you in.

Final Thought on Dating

Let it begin with you! Too often, we can be so focused on what we're looking for in our spouse that we forget to become the kind of individual worth looking for. The single years are incredible preparation for marriage; don't wait until you start dating to mature and deal with your dysfunctions; begin now to grow into the man or woman that is ready for marriage! You can't expect a top-shelf spouse if you're only committed to being a bottom-shelf person. Look at the list of qualities to look for in a future man or woman and begin to rate yourself on each one; then, with God and your church communities help, begin to grow into that list! The more you conform to God's Word and His Will, the more you'll attract the incredible spouse that God has in mind for you!

We're praying you find love as deep and rich,
and fulfilling as we have! There's nothing on earth like a
healthy and fulfilling marriage!

Make sure to tag us in your
proposal photos so we can celebrate with you!

ABOUT THE AUTHORS

Samuel is a passionate follower of Jesus, in love with his beautiful wife, Katie, and loves being a father to his two incredible girls, Mercedes and Kenzie. He and his wife are a part of the pastoral team at Awaken Church in San Diego, CA. They also serve the broader Church community through a discipleship resource called, "Following Jesus" and by preaching and ministering with a prophetic edge!

To connect with Samuel and Katie or for any ministry inquiries, contact them at the key sites or scan the QR code:
samueldeuth.com
preachingforward.com
followingjesusbook.com

Made in the USA
Middletown, DE
16 February 2025